WOMAN
in the
Wild

WOMAN
in the
Wild

The Everywoman's Guide to Hiking, Camping, and Backcountry Travel

SUSAN JOY PAUL

GUILFORD, CONNECTICUT

FALCON®

An imprint of The Rowman & Littlefield Publishing Group, Inc.
4501 Forbes Blvd., Ste. 200
Lanham, MD 20706
www.rowman.com
Falcon and FalconGuides are registered trademarks and Make Adventure
Your Story is a trademark of The Rowman & Littlefield Publishing Group, Inc.

Distributed by NATIONAL BOOK NETWORK

British Library Cataloguing in Publication Information available

Library of Congress Cataloging-in-Publication Data

Names: Paul, Susan Joy, author.
Title: Woman in the wild : the everywoman's guide to hiking, camping, and
   backcountry travel / Susan Joy Paul.
Description: Guilford, Connecticut : Falcon, 2021. | Includes index. |
   Summary: "Adventurer and guidebook author Susan Joy Paul provides real
   instruction for women of all ages and skill levels, from beginners to
   intermediate hikers and experienced mountaineers. She shares details
   gleaned from two decades of training and real-world experience, bringing
   together everything a woman needs to know to be safe, independent, and
   self-reliant at camp and on the trail"— Provided by publisher.
Identifiers: LCCN 2020047862 (print) | LCCN 2020047863 (ebook) | ISBN
   9781493049745 (paperback) | ISBN 9781493049745 (epub)
Subjects: LCSH: Outdoor recreation for women—Handbooks, manuals, etc. |
   Outdoor life—Handbooks, manuals, etc.
Classification: LCC GV191.64 .P38 2021 (print) | LCC GV191.64 (ebook) |
   DDC 796.5082—dc23
LC record available at https://lccn.loc.gov/2020047862
LC ebook record available at https://lccn.loc.gov/2020047863

♾™ The paper used in this publication meets the minimum requirements
of American National Standard for Information Sciences—Permanence of
Paper for Printed Library Materials, ANSI/NISO Z39.48-1992.

For every woman who fell in love with the wild and every woman who aspires to

Hiking with friends adds a layer of experience and skill while building camaraderie. Hikers head into Colorado's Collegiate Peaks in Chaffee County.

PHOTO BY QTINA FOX

Contents

Next Steps

Depending on the water depth, temperature, current, and creek bed terrain, stream crossings can vary from tricky to dangerous. On her way to Wind River Peak in Wyoming's Wind River Range, Jean Aschenbrenner hangs her boots around her neck, dons Tevas, and uses her trekking poles for balance. PHOTO BY KEN NOLAN

Acknowledgments

I HAD MANY hiking and climbing partners and mentors over the years—too many to list, or even remember. But I'd be sorely remiss if I didn't call out Douglas Hatfield, my hiking buddy for several years. Doug's technical and personal skills made him the perfect backcountry partner, mentor, and friend.

I had some help with this book. Alyson Kirk, Andrea Sansone, Beth Balser, Daria Holler, Geimi Chism, Teresa Gergen, Ellen Kerchner, Jean Aschenbrenner, Jennifer Roach, Leigh (Sug) Peterson, Linda Parobek, Lisa Heckel, Marsha Hawk, and Otina Fox provided photos and inspirational profiles. Several of these women also read some of the chapters in this book and gave me feedback to help make it better. Mountain Chalet of Colorado Springs let me borrow their gear and clothing for photos, Stewart M. Green took the gear shots, and Carolyn McNeil lent her Photoshopping skills to the project.

I also got a lot of support from my acquiring editor, Katie O'Dell; production editor Meredith Dias; copyeditor Melissa Hayes; layout artist Rhonda Baker; and proofreader Beth Richards.

Finally, this book wouldn't have been written if it weren't for David Quinn, who got my proposal in front of Jessica d'Arbonne, and if Jess hadn't believed in it. These two, along with David Legere, Ryan Meyer, and everyone at FalconGuides, deserve a whole lot of credit. Thank you, all.

Backcountry goals motivate you to get out more, go farther, and go higher. Otina Fox skins toward the east face of Colorado's Huron Peak on her quest to ski all of that state's 14,000-foot peaks.
PHOTO COURTESY OF OTINA FOX

Introduction

WHEN I WROTE the first book proposal for *Woman in the Wild* in 2011, I couldn't get a publisher. I was told the market was too small. *Women aren't really interested in the outdoors*, they said. *You need a broader market.* That didn't make sense to me because *I* was interested, and I was seeing other women hiking the trails, climbing the crags, and scrambling to mountaintops. But their numbers were still low, and I wondered why. *Why weren't there as many women as men in the wild?*

Fortunately, I got a contract for another book, and then another, and another—guidebooks to Colorado's hot springs, waterfalls, and mountains. After the books were published, libraries and visitor centers invited me to do presentations. So I did. And I noticed something about my audiences: They were almost all women. If so many women were interested in getting outside, why weren't more of them out there?

Talking to them after the presentations, I got my answer. They wanted to explore the backcountry, but they didn't know where to start. Some had joined hiking groups that hadn't worked out. The people who ran them tended to take a militant approach to the whole experience. There was an overriding sense of competition, with the experienced members held in high regard, while people new to the outdoors were looked down on and even castigated for not learning the skills fast enough, not being strong enough, or not being fast enough. These women didn't want to compete—they just wanted to learn how to enjoy the backcountry safely and without getting lost. I believed them, because I'd encountered similar situations when I started out: hiking groups led by gruff, overbearing taskmasters who thought their job was to whip you into shape and put you down when you didn't measure up to their standards. I was lucky enough to find people who *didn't* treat women this way, or I, too, may have given up on the backcountry.

Another issue some women had was not having anyone in these groups to ask about sensitive topics, like how to go to the bathroom outside or deal with their period. In fact, they didn't even know who to ask for advice on benign subjects like hair and skin care and personal hygiene on long trips. Men didn't deal with these things, it seemed, and other women tended to shame them for even asking. The unspoken message was, "Woman up! If you want to enjoy the backcountry, start acting like a man or else stay home."

Outside of groups and clubs, the information women wanted was scattered in books and internet articles, but there was no one place to find the answers to their questions. Much of what *was* available was sorely behind the times. I knew this was true, because when I wrote that first book proposal in 2011, I had researched the "competition." Most of the books were written for men, and the women's books were packed with camping recipes, games to play with your kids, and tips for looking good for your man.

By 2019, the outdoor industry was starting to come around, but I still heard from women who wanted a reliable source of backcountry information. And I still didn't have a contract for this book. At the Outdoor Retailer Winter Show in Denver, a conversation changed that. Someone from a publishing house asked me how I got into guidebook writing, and I told him about my proposal—and how it had bombed. He asked if I'd mind him mentioning the book idea to an editor friend. A few weeks later, I had a contract with FalconGuides.

I learned about the backcountry by taking a lot of courses, reading a lot of books, and through decades of experience. I had some terrific mentors along the way. And I finally wrote down what I know to help other women, sharing the knowledge I've gained from hundreds of hikes, climbs, and mountaineering adventures in this book.

The first section, *Backcountry Essentials*, covers the basics like finding places to go and people to go with. There are chapters on clothing, gear, packing for a trip, and camping and cooking. *You in the Wild* covers the personal stuff: nutrition, hydration, and hygiene. There are chapters on staying healthy and what to do if you get sick or injured. Next is the technical section, *Pushing Off*, which explains how to use a map and compass and other navigational tools. You'll also learn about the different types of terrain and weather you might run into, how to be a responsible citizen out there, and how to stay out of trouble. *Reaching New Heights* is packed with ideas for taking your adventures to a new level with training, leadership skills, working toward goals, planning your own trips, and setting yourself up for success. Finally, *Next Steps* introduces high-altitude mountaineering, winter hiking and camping, glacier travel, rock climbing, ice climbing, and international trips. These advanced topics each deserve their own books. You will need more instruction to pursue the technically demanding activities, but there is enough information to whet your appetite for adventure and encourage you to keep learning and practicing to go as big, hard, and high as you want.

Sprinkled among the chapters are profiles of women in the wild who enjoy the backcountry as much as I do—maybe more. These are not professional athletes. They're women like you and me, with families, careers, and a passion for the wild.

I'm not an athlete. In fact, I flunked gym in high school and smoked cigarettes for years. But once I discovered backcountry travel, everything changed. I got in shape, and finally quit smoking while training for an unguided trip with seven men up Mount Rainier. The thought of causing my rope team to turn around short of the summit because I wasn't fit enough to continue motivated me to quit. I gave up smoking, trained hard, did the climb, and never looked back. I did other hikes, climbs, and mountaineering trips, too, with friends, mentors, and solo. I got up high in Colorado, Wyoming, Utah, and California, and traveled to Mexico and South America to climb even higher. I still have many more adventures ahead, but I had to write this book first so other women can learn from my experiences.

This book will give you everything you need to get started in the backcountry, and lots of insider info from someone who's been there. But it's just the beginning. Once you take steps to become a woman in the wild, you'll want to seek your own experiences. Read more, take courses, and find people to learn with, and from. And get out there. Because a woman in the wild is the best kind of woman to be.

The author on the approach to Vermilion Peak, the highpoint of San Juan County, Colorado.

BACKCOUNTRY ESSENTIALS

Caroline Moore takes in views of Grizzly Peak D after descending the northwest ridge of Lenawee Mountain above Arapahoe Basin, Colorado.
PHOTO BY OTINA FOX

Daria Holler gets into the backcountry as often as she can and often guides others in the Wind River Range and Grand Canyon.
PHOTO BY AUSTIN HOLLER

CHAPTER 1

GETTING STARTED

YOUR REASONS for being in the wild are up to you. You might have a destination in mind. Maybe you want to get some outdoor exercise. You could be looking to make new friends around a healthy activity. If you're new to the wild, think about why you want to get out there and what you want to gain from the experience.

If you have less than a day to get out, consider a *day hike*, where you drive to the trailhead, hike, and drive home. Or you can stay at a campground and enjoy *car camping*. If you're looking to do multiday hikes, you can try *backpacking*, where you carry more gear, set up a tent every night, and prepare your own food. In this chapter, we'll talk about the basics—where and when to hike and who's going to join you on your outings.

YOUR BACKCOUNTRY BUDDIES

Some women treasure the solitude and independence of hiking alone. Others prefer the companionship, shared expertise, and safety of going with others. The company you keep on the trail can have a major impact on your experience.

Hiking with Other People

Hiking with others adds another layer of knowledge and skill. You and your hiking buddies share responsibilities such as trip planning, driving, route finding, and carrying shared gear. If you're camping with other people, you can work together to filter water, set up tents, and cook meals. When you're starting out, look at your circle of friends to see who would be interested in taking this journey with you. No matter how many books you read—including this one—nothing beats the skills gained from actual hiking and camping trips.

You can also join a hiking group. The American Hiking Society's Alliance of Hiking Organizations is a network of various land, trail, and hiking groups and clubs that cater to hikers at all experience levels. The Sierra Club has chapters around the country that offer local and international trips. Joining a local hikers' Meetup or Facebook group is another way to find people in your area to hike with, and many outdoor websites have threads dedicated to locating hiking buddies.

Organized hiking groups often stipulate a minimum number of people on an outing. Some groups require at least four hikers so that if one gets sick or injured, a second person can stay with them while the other two go for help. This way, no one person is ever alone. Groups may require a hike leader to guide the group and a secondary leader to ensure that no one is left behind. Who you hike with is a personal decision, but consider your health, experience, and level of comfort with your choice. You might start off by going with an organized group and getting to know the people in it. Later, you and others within the group who have similar outdoor goals may form your own informal hiking partnership or group.

Solo Hiking

When you hike by yourself, you have to make all the decisions about where to go, how to get there, and when to turn around. You are solely responsible for your own safety. Self-sufficiency is a good skill to have, but it is especially critical for people who hike solo. If you get sick or injured, you have to take care of yourself. The hiking experience is different, too. There's no conversation, and for some people, having no one to talk to is uncomfortable. This isn't true for every person; some hikers prefer solitude. Hiking solo is not for everyone. If you're not fully prepared to do the hike by yourself, seek out hiking partners. If you do decide to go it alone, research the route and let someone know where you're going.

WHERE TO GO

If you're new to hiking and camping and aren't ready to figure it all out by yourself, start by going on outings set up by someone else, such as the leader of a hiking group. Whoever organized the hike did some research and found a suitable route. It's okay to take advantage of their work, but do some of your own research, too. If the hike organizer provides a map or directions to the trailhead, study them. Figure out where the trailhead is from your home and what roads you'll be on. On the map, look for the names of national or state parks, wilderness areas, trails, rivers, and lakes.

If the hike leader provides you with a topographical map and you know how to read it, study the land. Is it steep or mostly level? From the trailhead, will you be hiking north, south, east, or west? Are there any important trail junctions along the route? Do an internet search on the name of the trailhead and read up on the area. Check the weather report so you know what to wear and carry in your pack.

Many people who join hiking groups don't do any research at all. They show up expecting the organizer to be their tour guide, and that's not what being a woman in the wild is about. Are you a tourist or an active participant? There's a big difference, and it starts with your attitude and how you approach and prepare for every outing.

Start Local

If you're ready to go on your own hikes, whether alone or with friends, look for somewhere close by. You might already have a place in mind, or you can pick up a guidebook to get ideas. FalconGuides has hundreds of hiking books covering areas countrywide. Head to their website or to your local bookstore or outdoor retailer and see what catches your eye. Starting out, you might like destination hikes to places like lakes and waterfalls. This gives you something to look forward to. As you read about each hike, pay close attention to details like distance, elevation gain, and difficulty. If you can't find a hike you like in a book, go online and search for local, state, and national parks; national forests and monuments; Bureau of Land Management (BLM) lands; and wilderness areas that you'd like to visit.

Next, pick up a *DeLorme Atlas & Gazetteer* for your state. This is the big red book of maps you've probably seen in a rack at the gas station. Though we've come a long way with digital maps and GPS devices, a physical map book for trip planning gives you a big-picture view of land areas across your state for a better perspective of where you are in relation to your destination. This isn't the kind of manual you'd carry in a pack; use it to plan your hikes, and bring it along in the car to reference along the way.

Once you've decided where you want to hike, research the area. If the location has a website, look for information, including trail systems, restrictions, and seasonal closures, and see if there are any maps to download. You can also download US Geological Survey (USGS) quadrangle maps from that organization's website and purchase National Geographic *Trails Illustrated* topographical maps online and from outdoor recreation shops and bookstores. Chapter 19 on "Trip Planning" covers this topic in more detail.

Daria Holler strolls through the Grand Canyon, a popular hiking destination.
PHOTO BY AUSTIN HOLLER

DARIA HOLLER has been passionate about getting others into the wilderness and sharing the experience with them since college. Whether it's mountains, rock, trees, trail, on foot or bike, she has been climbing for as long as she can remember. Daria has climbed Cotopaxi, Ecuador's highest active volcano, cycled across the United States twice, and cycled the California coast to raise funding and awareness to fight injustice. She has guided many teams into the backcountry of Wyoming's Wind River Range and Arizona's Grand Canyon. Daria loves big trees and sleeping on the Esplanade of the Grand Canyon under a canvas of stars.

WHEN TO GO

Many women enjoy the backcountry year-round, in all seasons and weather conditions. If you're new to hiking, go when the weather's pleasant. As you become more experienced, you'll toughen up—mentally and physically—while also getting a better handle on the appropriate clothing, gear, and skills needed for any conditions.

Start off with hikes that begin and end during the daylight hours. As you get more accustomed to moving on trail—and you've invested in a headlamp and extra batteries—you can extend your hikes into darkness.

Check the weather report for your destination several days before your hike and check it again each day leading up to the hike. The National Oceanic and Atmospheric Administration (NOAA) website has extended forecasts for locations countrywide where you can find out the predicted temperature highs and lows, humidity, wind speed and direction, visibility, wind chill, and precipitation.

KEEP LEARNING, PAY IT FORWARD, AND GIVE BACK

If you enjoy hiking, continue your education beyond this book. Pay it forward to the outdoor community and give back to the environment. Read more books and watch videos on camping, hiking, and backcountry travel. Take formal classes and attend lectures. Seek out mentors, hire professional guides, and practice regularly to hone your skills. As you become an accomplished woman in the wild, invite other women to join you. Become a mentor to someone who wants to learn and has no one to teach them. Look for groups in your area that support women and girls and share your knowledge in a classroom or on a trail.

Volunteer opportunities—such as trail building, trail cleanup, and leading hikes for nonprofit organizations—can be found everywhere. You can also join a "friends of" group associated with a local park or open space. Giving back enriches your experience and lightens your footprint in the wild.

TAKE STEPS

1. Find a local hiking group and sign up for an outing. If you like the group, consider joining it, and if you don't, try another group.
2. Find an area you'd like to explore on your own or with a friend—a park, forest, or other public land. Do some research: Download a map of the trail system, pick a trailhead and trail, and figure out how to get there.
3. Check the weather and pick a day to do your hike.

Ellen Kerchner dresses for cold air and sunshine on a backcountry ski trip.

CHAPTER 2

WHAT TO WEAR

COMFORT, DURABILITY, AND SAFETY are key when it comes to back-country clothing. Choose clothes that fit well, feel good, and are suitable for the conditions.

LAYERING

In the backcountry, expect to add and remove clothing to adjust to changing conditions. *Layering*—where you wear the lightest layer next to your skin, then add insulating and protective layers—allows you to dress for varying weather without stripping down to bare skin.

Before you invest in clothing layers, start with the activewear in your closet and add pieces as you need them. Research the areas you're going

ELLEN KERCHNER is a Colorado native who grew up exploring the outdoors under the tutelage of two outdoor educator parents. She traveled the West via whitewater raft, horseback, mountain bike, and backcountry ski. Ellen splits her time between organic flower farming in the summer and working at her local outdoor gear shop in the winter. She is passionate about conservation and land management to restore working lands and protect wilderness in the West. Ellen believes that regenerative agriculture and outdoor recreation are means to the same end, creating meaningful ties between people and place, leading to more intentional use of land. She hopes that more women start farming and exploring our beautiful Western landscapes!

to explore to get an idea of the fabrics that work best for the temperatures, precipitation, and humidity. Fibers and finishes change from year to year as manufacturers seek to provide high-performing, lightweight, comfortable clothing. Talk to your local outdoor clothing retailer for the latest recommendations. Then try on the clothes. Shopping online may be convenient, but there is nothing like trying things on to make sure you have the perfect fit, fabric, and design you're looking for. Build your wardrobe slowly, selecting pieces only as you need them to ensure pieces fit together and to avoid wasting money on items you'll never wear.

FOOTWEAR

Your first and most important purchase should be footwear. Feet take a beating on the trail and you have to take care of them. Choose shoes and boots with support tailored to *your* foot, a grippy sole, and a comfortable footbed—the cushioning insole that protects the soles of your feet and affects the fit. When shopping for shoes, take other people's opinions with a grain of salt. A hiking shoe that's perfect for one person may not fit your foot at all. Some styles are narrow and others are wide through the ankle and toebox, with varying levels of ankle and arch support.

Before you buy any shoes or boots, try them on with the socks you expect to wear with them. Wear them around the store. Some retailers have multiple levels with steps that you can run up and down, or ramps to walk on. A tight boot that rubs or a loose one that allows your foot to shift can lead to blisters and lost toenails. Once you find a brand that works for your foot, you may find that all footwear by that company suits you.

Footwear for the Trail

The type of footwear you need depends on the terrain. If you hike on dry trails, a pair of *trail runners* will do. They're lightweight, breathable, and have a cushioned footbed and grippy sole. Trail runners may not be the best choice for wet or rocky terrain. The low-cut style doesn't provide ankle protection or support, and can allow twigs, dirt, and scree into the shoe. Trail runners usually aren't waterproof, either, so if the trail is muddy or there's a chance of rain, consider wearing something else.

One step up from trail runners are *hiking shoes*. These provide more support, and some are waterproof. They're also stiffer and heavier than trail runners.

Choose from mountaineering boots, hiking boots, hiking shoes, and trail runners, depending on your adventure.

Next are *hiking boots*, which provide ankle protection and stability. Like hiking shoes, some boots are waterproof. The higher cut helps keep water and debris from getting inside. Hiking boots are a good choice for wet or rocky trails and for uneven terrain like talus and boulders. They're usually stiffer than shoes, so they keep your foot from getting sore and tired from flexing on uneven terrain. The extra support is ideal for backpacking, where you're hiking for many miles with a heavy pack and a lot of pressure on your feet. Hiking boots come in different levels of insulation and support for hiking, backpacking, and mountaineering.

Socks

Buy socks for the weather, terrain, and your shoe. In warm weather, one pair of lightweight hiking socks is fine. Your socks should be higher than the collar of your footwear to protect your skin. They should be made of fabric that wicks moisture and dries quickly. Stay away from cotton socks, which take a long time to dry and lose their insulating ability when wet.

In cooler weather, wear heavier hiking or backpacking socks to keep your feet warm. Backpacking socks provide more cushion for your soles, too. Sock liners, worn under your socks, are an option for added comfort

While wool socks are a longtime favorite, vegan synthetics are rising in popularity. Choose the right weight for the adventure.

and warmth. Examine your socks every season and replace them if they're worn out so you don't end up with cold feet or blisters.

Footwear Add-Ons

Dirt and gravel can get into your hiking shoes and rub against your ankles and the soles of your feet. On dry, loose trails, add a pair of low- or mid-rise gaiters to prevent debris from slipping in. On snow, high winter gaiters keep your lower legs and feet dry. These are strips of fabric, typically nylon or Gore-Tex, that wrap around your lower legs and fasten with Velcro and a buckle. Winter gaiters keep your pants dry and cover your boots so snow doesn't get in.

Traction includes crampons, strap-on spikes such as MICROSpikes, and other devices that attach to your boots to grip hard snow and ice. If you plan to wear traction, make sure it fits your boot size and type. Some boots are specially made to hold a crampon.

Sole inserts tucked into footwear provide a custom fit, arch support, and heel stabilization. Adding inserts requires that you remove the shoe manufacturer's insole, so you could be sacrificing cushion for fit. Before you take this step, weigh the benefits and get a professional fit.

Unless all your hikes are on dry ground, buy waterproof footwear or get some waterproofing solution and apply as needed.

Mid-rise, waterproof gaiters made of Gore-Tex keep water and debris out of shoes while MICROspikes provide traction on icy trails. GEAR COURTESY OF KAHTOOLA

Footwear at Camp

At camp, get out of your hiking shoes and rest your feet. Sandals with grippy soles work well in warm weather. As the temperature drops, add a pair of socks. Sandals, slides, or plastic clogs with socks may not be the best fashion choice, but the combination is warm and comfortable. In cold weather, opt for insulated booties. These are lightweight, puffy booties with durable soles that keep your feet warm and dry and are suitable for limited outdoor wear. You'll appreciate booties when you leave the tent in the middle of the night to go to the bathroom. Sandals and booties are also comfortable choices for the drive home.

TOPS AND BOTTOMS

Layered shirts, pants, vests, and jackets protect your torso and legs and allow you to adjust your clothes for changing weather, temperatures, and your own body heat. Hiking clothes generally come in three types: a base layer that you wear next to your skin; an insulating layer for warmth; and a protective layer to guard against wind and precipitation. Depending on conditions, you may need several insulating layers. Clothing layers can be worn over underwear, but some—like running shorts and sports bras—have their own built-in, next-to-skin support.

Base Layers

Base layers are thin, breathable tops and bottoms that wick moisture away from your skin. In warm weather, think sports bra or tank top and bike pants; short-sleeved shirt and shorts; or long-sleeved lightweight shirt and hiking pants. You may have activewear clothing for the gym, yoga, or another sport that works fine as a summer-weight base layer. As you start spending more time in the backcountry, look for base layers made especially for hiking. Some are made from fabrics that repel insects or protect you from the sun. Others are convertible, such as pants with zip-off legs. A summer base layer may be all you need for your hike but carry extra layers in your pack, such as a warm shirt or rain jacket for changing conditions.

In colder weather, your base layer insulates you from the cold while wicking away moisture. Think stretchy, form-fitting long underwear. Unlike summer base layers, winter base layers aren't worn alone, but form the base for other layers.

Insulating Layers

Insulating layers for cooler temperatures should fit comfortably over your base layers. For torso, a fleece top with a high collar or hood and a three-quarter zip makes a nice layer. You can adjust the zipper to suit your body temperature without worrying about it coming undone at the bottom. For legs, hiking pants over a form-fitting base layer work well. In very cold weather, wear insulated pants. Some insulated pants are water- and wind-resistant, a plus for wet or windy hikes.

Protective Layers

Softshell and hardshell protective layers provide a partial or full barrier against wind, rain, and snow. *Softshells* are soft on your skin—warm and insulating on the inside and wind- and water-resistant on the outside—but not waterproof. Softshell shirts, pants, vests, and jackets with or without hoods are a comfortable choice for added warmth and weather

Pants, zippered tops, and jackets can be layered for changing conditions.

resistance. *Hardshells* are stiffer and less comfortable but more durable and waterproof.

The most common hardshell layer is a hooded rain jacket. Jackets long enough to cover your butt will keep you drier but tend to cost more. If you can't afford a decent rain jacket, you should at least carry a hooded rain poncho, available at most retailers for a few bucks. Then save up for a good jacket. Look for one with "zipped pits"—zippers under the armpits—for adjustable ventilation on hot, wet hikes. Test the hood to make sure it covers your head and test the closure to make sure it's easy to fasten.

Rain pants keep your hiking pants dry in wet weather and in tall, dewy grass. They usually have an elasticized waist that stretches over your hiking pants, and some have full- or half-zip legs, making it easier to slip them over your boots. Rain jackets and pants are useful when you're hiking through areas with dense, prickly brush, or near standing water where insects swarm. Briars, burrs, and mosquitoes are less likely to cling to the protective fabric. Make sure your rain jacket and pants fit over all your other clothes.

Test all zippers, snaps, straps, buttons, and ties to make sure they work well and are easy to reach and manipulate. You may be dressing in high winds, in the dark, in pouring rain or blinding snow. For cold winter clothing, test the closures wearing glove liners. You should never have to bare your hands to add a layer in the backcountry. If a zipper tag is too small to grab with your gloves on, loop a length of nylon cord to the end to create a longer pull.

For very cold temps, you'll need a puffy, insulated jacket with a hood. Puffy jackets come in both down-filled and vegan, synthetic options. This type of jacket will typically sit at the bottom of your pack for the duration of your hike, but if you're resting on a cold mountaintop or at camp for a while, you'll need it to avoid getting chilled.

HEAD AND HANDS

Skin that's exposed to sun, wind, and precipitation is susceptible to sunburn, windburn, and frostbite. When it comes to protective accessories for your head and hands, you have a lot of options.

Hats, Headbands, and Ear Warmers

Have at least two hats: a lightweight brimmed hat to protect your face from the sun, and a snug-fitting fleece or knit cap to keep your head warm. Your brimmed hat should be made from a fabric that dries quickly; if it gets sweaty, your head will get cold. Some brimmed hats have a neck flap to protect your neck and ears from sunburn.

Brimmed caps keep the sun out of your eyes.

Knit or fleece caps, buffs, and headbands keep your head, face, and ears warm.

For your warm cap, go with a fabric that dries quickly and retains its insulating qualities when wet. You can add a separate headband or ear warmers to keep your hair out of your face, protect your ears from wind and cold, and "seal off" the sides of your hat so cold air doesn't sneak in around your temples. In extreme cold and wind, pull your jacket hood over your hat for another layer of warmth and protection.

Eyewear

Sunglasses protect your eyes from UV (ultraviolet) radiation damage from the sun, prevent snow blindness, and may guard against cataracts. Eye protection is especially important at high altitude where there is little shade and for back-country travel on snow, when the sun is beating down on you from above and reflecting off the ground. Invest in sunglasses with polycarbonate lenses and a UV rating of 400 to block UVA/UVB

Geimi Chism protects her face and eyes with a brimmed hat and sunglasses.

radiation. Sunglasses should cover your eyes completely and wrap around your temples so no light can leak in on the sides.

Neckwear

No matter how well-dressed you are for the weather, a stiff breeze down the front of your shirt will chill you to the bone. Wear a *buff* around your neck to keep out the cold. Unlike a scarf that has to be wrapped or tied, a buff, balaclava, or neck gaiter is a stretchy loop of fabric that slips over your head and clings around your neck. Buffs come in a variety of weights and can be reconfigured into different face, head, and neck coverings. In cold weather, a buff pulled up over your nose not only keeps your face warmer, it also creates a warm layer of air for breathing, so you're not sucking cold air into your lungs. In high desert winds, a buff prevents sand from getting into your nose and mouth. Raise and lower the buff to eat and drink. As the day warms up, remove your buff from your neck and loop it around your wrist to wipe your sweaty face or dripping nose. Have at least one light buff for summer and a heavier one for winter, and double up on them in extremely cold temperatures.

Gloves

Fingers and hands, with their high ratio of surface area to mass, are more susceptible to wind and cold than other parts of the body. Ears, feet,

Gloves and glove liners add warmth and prevent skin damage and frostbite.

noses, and toes are also susceptible but can be covered with hats, face-masks, buffs, and footwear—protection that doesn't have to be removed. Since you use your hands to adjust clothing, eat, drink, and go to the bathroom, you're likely to remove your gloves and expose your hands and fingers to cold, wind, and moisture.

Like other clothing systems, gloves can be layered for extra protection. In cool conditions, a glove *liner* is all you need. The glove liners should be thin and flexible enough to allow you to do whatever you need without taking them off. In colder temps, add a second, insulating glove. These are thicker, bulkier, and a lot warmer than glove liners. Try them on over the liner for the best fit.

TAKE STEPS

1. Figure out where you want to go and the kind of clothing you'll need for the environment and conditions.
2. Sort through your wardrobe for clothing that you already own to repurpose for these initial adventures. Make a list of what else you need for your first hikes and do some online research to get a sense of variety and prices.
3. Visit the outdoor retailers in your area. Find one with knowledgeable employees, a good selection of clothing, and prices within your budget.

The bigger the adventure, the more you may have to pack. Andrea Sansone warms up in a sleeping bag before sorting food, clothing, and gear on a campout in the Weminuche Wilderness of southwest Colorado. PHOTO BY ANDREW HAMILTON

CHAPTER 3

WHAT TO PACK

WHAT YOU CARRY in your pack depends on where you're going and for how long. This chapter covers the basics for any outing. Additional gear for car camping, backpacking, and adventures on mixed terrain is covered in subsequent chapters. Of course, you'll need a pack to put everything in, and we'll talk about that in chapter 4, "How to Pack." First, let's talk about the essentials.

THE TWELVE ESSENTIALS

A woman in the wild's packing list starts with the traditional ten essentials and adds a toilet kit and extra gear for the terrain. After a hike, examine your twelve essentials and see what needs to be recharged, replenished, or replaced before your next adventure.

Extra Clothing

In addition to the clothes you wear on your hike, figure out what other clothing you might need if the weather changes. It may not be raining when you start your hike, but if there's any chance of precipitation, you'll want to pack a jacket. Check the weather report for temperature and weather predictions for your start time and dress accordingly. Look at the predictions for the span of time that you'll be outside and pack whatever else you'll need, such as extra gloves, hats, jackets, and fleece tops. If you're going to be crossing streams, consider carrying an extra pair of socks. Hiking in wet shoes and socks can lead to blisters. For trips with a lot of stream crossings, you could even add a pair of lightweight water shoes and neoprene socks that dry quickly to prevent your boots from getting soaked.

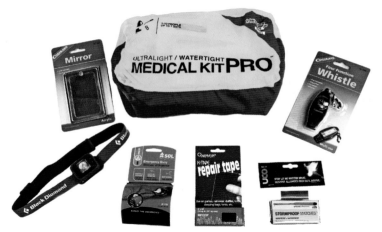

Essentials like a first-aid kit, headlamp, and emergency shelter are staples for a woman in the wild's pack.

Hydration

Hydration in the form of water and other drinks can be carried in a bladder inside your pack with a tube for drinking on the go, in bottles in your pack, and in an insulated container—especially nice for hot soup, cocoa, or tea. You'll want something to drink for the drive up and back and for the trail. See chapter 6, "Water and Hydration," for more on this topic.

Nutrition

Pack enough food for the drive and for the hike. A combination of sweet and salty foods like dried fruit, bars, nuts, and jerky are particularly appealing on long hikes, but if you're planning to stop on the trail for lunch, you'll appreciate traditional food like a sandwich or a wrap. Chapter 7 on "Food and Nutrition" covers this topic.

Toilet Kit

You will rarely have access to a restroom in the backcountry, so pack a toilet kit. Chapter 8, "Personal Care," provides information about your toilet kit and how to use it. You can expand your toilet kit to make it a complete cleanup kit or make a separate kit for personal hygiene and grooming, also discussed in that chapter.

Sun Protection

Sun protection includes a hat to protect your face from the sun, sunglasses, and SPF 30 or higher sunscreen and lip balm. Sun protection is necessary year-round and in any weather. Chapter 9, "Staying Healthy," covers this topic in more detail.

First-Aid Kit

Your first-aid kit can be as basic or as complete as you want, but at a minimum, include whatever medications you're on. Chapter 10 includes a discussion of basic first-aid measures and a checklist so you can build your own kit.

Fire Starter

Fire starter—a lighter, matches, and kindling—are typically packed in a cooking kit, but if you wind up on an unplanned bivouac, you may have to start a fire to keep warm. A lighter or waterproof matches along with some kindling will spark a flame, and you'll have to feed it with dry, dead branches to keep it going. You can buy kindling at your local gear shop or go the cheaper route of carrying some cotton balls soaked in petroleum jelly in a film-canister-sized waterproof container.

Headlamp

An easy trail in daylight can be difficult and even impossible to follow in the dark. A headlamp lights your path before sunrise and after sunset. Carry extra batteries and know how to replace them before you head out. If the batteries in your headlamp go dead, replace them by the light of a friend's headlamp. If you hike solo, carry two headlamps so you won't have to swap out batteries in the dark. Have a system for packing your batteries so you can tell the used and fresh ones apart. This might be as simple as a double baggy with the interior bag for fresh batteries and the outer bag for depleted ones.

Navigation System

Depending on the trip and available information, pack a trail map, topo map, photocopy of guidebook pages, printout from a web page, or hand-written instructions describing your route—whatever you need to get from the trailhead to your destination and back without getting lost. Bring a pen or pencil to take notes while you hike. Carry a compass and know how to use it. You may also have a GPS or favorite navigation phone app. Map and compass orientation and land navigation are explained in chapter 11.

On a trip to Snowmass Mountain in Colorado's Elk Mountains, Andrea Sansone carries all the essentials plus extra gear for the rocky terrain. PHOTO BY ANDREW HAMILTON

ANDREA SANSONE is a nurse in a neonatal intensive care unit at Children's Hospital Colorado who fell in love with the outdoors in high school. She snowboards and splitboards during the winter months, but her true passion is hiking 14,000-foot mountains in the summer and fall. She holds the California 14er speed record for women, summiting all fifteen mountains with her partner, Andrew Hamilton, in August 2017 in 7 days, 11 hours, and 22 minutes. Andrea also traversed Colorado's Elk Range Centennials on foot in 70 hours, and in 2020, she set a new women's record for *Nolan's 14*, enchaining fourteen peaks over 14,000 feet in Colorado's Sawatch Range in 53 hours and 14 minutes, continuing on to Mount of the Holy Cross to make it a "Holy Nolan's" for a total of 140 miles on foot in 85 hours and 3 minutes. Andrea's favorite quote is the Chinese proverb, "Be not afraid of going slowly; be afraid only of standing still." She says, "It doesn't matter how fast you go or how strong you are; as long as you're constantly learning, growing, doing your best, and enjoying every experience and opportunity life throws at you, that's all that matters."

Emergency Shelter

If you end up having to stay put for a while, an emergency shelter, bivy sack, or "space blanket" to wrap yourself in or lie under adds a layer of protection and warmth against the elements.

Repair Kit

Outdoor adventure clothing and gear is built to withstand the rigors of backcountry travel, but clothing rips, zippers jam, and pack straps break. A basic repair kit includes duct tape, fishing line, zip ties, and scissors or a knife. A graphite pencil lead or waxy lip balm will smooth a sticky zipper on your pants or on your tent. Fishing line and duct tape hold a pair of glasses together in a pinch, and a zip tie replaces a busted shoelace. You can add an eyeglass repair kit and a small sewing kit to patch tears in clothing, sleeping bags, and tents. You may never use anything in your repair kit, but you'll be glad to have it if the need arises.

Extra Gear

Extra gear includes anything else you need for your specific hike. This includes a helmet, trekking poles, traction, snowshoes, ice axe, bug spray, and whatever else the terrain and environment demand. You don't have to buy all these items today; as you get out more, you'll figure out the kind of gear you need for your particular adventures. Extra gear is discussed more fully within its respective chapter (e.g., you'll find much more about camping and cooking gear in chapter 5; ice axes in chapter 22, "Winter in the Wilderness"; and harnesses in chapter 24, "Rock and Ice Climbing").

TAKE STEPS

1. Gather items for your own "twelve essentials." Make a place for them in your home so you can pack quickly for a hike. As you get more gear, this space might expand to a gear closet, gear wall, or an entire gear room.
2. Make a list of what else you think you'll need. Talk to friends, do some online and book research, and think about the kind of gear you might like to have.
3. Visit your local outdoor retailer and see what kinds of essential items they carry that you don't have. Talk to the people who work there about what they recommend for your needs and budget.

Jennifer Roach takes a break in Wyoming on her quest to complete the Continental Divide Trail through the United States.
PHOTO BY SUSAN COOPER

CHAPTER 4

HOW TO PACK

MOST OF YOUR clothing and gear will go on your body or in your pack. Items you'll probably want to put on at the trailhead can go into a duffel or gear bag. You might also have a cooler for food and drinks. Some snacks will go into your pack at the trailhead, while post-hike drinks like chocolate milk and foods like salty chips may be left behind in the cooler. You can make all these decisions as you pack. First, you need to get a pack.

WHAT KIND OF PACK DO I NEED?

When you're first starting out, it's fine to use whatever pack you have on hand. As you figure out the kinds of trips you prefer, zero in on the best pack for your trips. The most common types of packs are day packs and backpacks. If you're interested in specific activities beyond hiking, such as rock climbing, you can repurpose your day pack and backpack or invest in packs made specifically for those adventures.

> Packs come in a lot of fabrics, sizes, capacities, and configurations, but most have the same basic parts: A main compartment that makes up the body of the pack, holds most of your gear, and closes on top with a zipper or drawstring. Every part of your pack is attached to this main compartment.

> The "front" of the pack faces away from your body and the back of the pack faces toward you. To remember the difference, just think "back to back."

> A haul loop on top for hanging your pack, tying it into a rope, or picking it up with one hand

> Shoulder straps on the back of the pack that rest on your shoulders, aligning the pack with your body. On a day pack, the shoulder straps also support the weight of the pack.
> A hip belt that straps below your waist and rests on your hips. On a day pack, this is simply a strap that keeps the pack aligned with your body while on a backpack, the hip belt keeps most of the pack weight on your hips and off your shoulders.
> Exterior compartments on the outside of the pack:
>> Zippered pocket on top, in the pack's lid, for storing items you need to get to quickly or often, like maps, snacks, sunscreen, and toilet kit
>> Zippered pockets or open pouches on the front and sides of the pack for carrying items like a rain jacket or trekking poles
>> Zippered pockets or open pouches within the shoulder straps and hip belt for items like lip balm and snacks
> Interior compartments:
>> A second, zippered pouch under the pack's lid for items like car keys, batteries, and headlamps
>> A hydration pouch in the main compartment for a water bladder or hydration flask. If there's a hydration pouch, look for an opening near the top of the pack and loops on the shoulder straps to feed the bladder's tube to the front of the pack. (We'll talk about hydration systems in more detail in chapter 6.)
> Exterior straps and buckles that help align your pack with your body and keep the weight of the pack on your hips:
>> Load adjuster straps between the body of the pack and the shoulder straps
>> Vertical shoulder strap adjusters
>> A horizontal sternum strap that connects the shoulder straps across your chest
>> Stabilizer straps for adjusting the hip belt
>> Plastic or metal adjustable buckles for tailoring the fit of your pack to your body
> Interior and exterior compression straps and cords for adjusting the pack to its contents
> Exterior straps and loops that hold detachable pack parts, such as a second, separate lid

- Exterior loops for hanging a helmet, a GPS, an ice axe, a sleeping pad, and other items
- An interior key fob at the top of the main compartment or in the lid
- Backpacks may also have a lumbar pad and a ventilation panel to keep your back dry.
- Some packs have a rain cover that slips over the pack, or you may have to buy one. In a pinch, a garbage bag works well to keep your pack dry.

Day Packs

A day pack is big enough to hold everything you need for a day hike—your twelve essentials, including some clothing and gear. Day packs are usually soft and collapsible with no internal frame to support them. The size as it relates to capacity or volume (not your body size) varies from about 1,200 to 2,400 cubic inches, or 20 to 40 liters, and is made to haul up to 25 pounds of gear. If you don't need to carry any overnight gear or extra gear for mountaineering or climbing, a day pack is all you need.

Backpacks

A backpack is necessary for overnight trips where you're not car-camping. The pack fits all your essentials plus your camping gear, cooking gear, and food. It has a bigger main compartment, more support, and more features than a day pack. Backpacks usually have an internal frame or suspension system that maintains the shape of the pack even when it's not filled. Backpacks run about 2,400 to 5,200 cubic inches in volume, or about 40 to 85 liters. They carry more weight than a day pack, with the maximum weight varying by size and construction. The more consecutive nights you plan to spend in the backcountry, the more capacity you'll need for food and fuel for your stove. If you don't have access to lakes, streams, or snow, you'll need to carry more water, too. For extremely large or heavy loads, bigger packs and packs with external frames are available. Buy the kind

The back of a pack fits against your back and features shoulder straps, a hip belt, and a haul loop.

of pack you'll use most often. Over time, you can decide whether you need a second or third pack.

Packs for Mixed Terrain

Your pack can be repurposed for mountaineering, rock and ice climb-ing, and glacier travel, but if you get involved in these activities, you may want to get different packs for each sport. For climbing on rock, a smaller, lighter pack with a slimmer profile and fewer or no side straps is preferred so it doesn't snag on rocks and brush. If you have to haul a lot of climbing gear to a crag or ice wall, a backpack works better. For ice climbers, look for loops and straps on the outside of the pack for anchoring your ice tools, axe, and helmet. Winter mountaineers should make sure the pack is large enough to hold an avalanche shovel. Some mountaineers carry a summit pack in addition to their backpack, leaving the backpack behind in the tent while they carry the smaller, lighter sum-mit pack from camp to summit. If you think you might be doing some overnight trips that include peak bagging (hiking to a lot of mountain-tops), look for a backpack that fits everything you need for an overnight trip but compresses to a smaller size and has a removable lid so you can transform it from backpack to summit pack.

Getting Fitted for Your Pack

Before you get fitted for a pack, decide what you're going to use it for and how big the main compartment needs to be to carry all your gear. Then check out all the different packs available in your price range. Do some online "window shopping" to get an idea of what's out there before heading to your favorite outdoor retailer for a fitting.

Things to look at are style, fabric, colors, features, weight, and, of course, capacity. There is no hard-and-fast rule for correlating pack capacity to days in the wilderness because everyone's gear is different. The best way to make sure you get a pack that's the right size for you is to throw everything you're bringing on a hike—essentials, clothing, extra gear, camping and cooking items, and food and drink, or similar-sized items—into a big garbage bag and take it with you to the store to get fit-ted for your pack. If you get a pack that's too small, you won't be able to carry all your stuff; too big, and you'll be carrying extra weight in the form of fabric, straps, and buckles. Let the store clerk know what you're carry-ing into the store, so they don't think you're shoplifting. You only have to do this one time and then you'll know exactly what size pack you'll need every time you go shopping for a new one. If you're buying a backpack and think you might want to buy a day pack down the road, get fitted for both so you don't have to carry all that stuff into the store with you again.

Women's packs are comparatively shorter, narrower, and lighter than men's and some models have shoulder straps and hip belts that are contoured to accommodate a woman's fuller bust and hips. In addition to the usual blues, greens, browns, and grays, women's packs are more likely to be offered in colors associated with femininity, like pink, purple, and teal. Check out all the women's packs and if you don't find one you like, look at the men's. Getting the right fit is most important when shopping for a pack.

Backpack sizes don't correlate with clothing sizes. They're based on the length of your torso from your C7 vertebra to the point where your iliac crest meets your spinal column. Any decent outdoor shop will have a tape measure on hand to fit you for a pack, but just in case, have a friend measure you before you head out the door. The C7 is that bony bump at the base of your neck, so have them hold the end of the tape measure there. To find your iliac crest, put your hands on your waist with your thumbs facing to the back, press down firmly on your hips, then slide your thumbs straight back. Extend the tape measure to where your thumbs meet at your spine. Write the number down and bring it with you to the store.

Find a pack in your size, capacity, and price range that has the features you want. Some backpacks have an adjustable suspension system that expands and contracts for different torso lengths, which makes sense if you're still growing or if you can't get a perfect fit for your size.

If the store clerk knows how to fit it to your body, you can let them help you make all the strap adjustments. If they don't know how to do this, do it yourself. Make sure the pack fits with the least and most amount of clothing you'll be wearing on a hike. If you don't have a coat with you, grab one off the rack and try the pack on while you're wearing it just to be sure you're getting the right fit. You want to make sure your pack is the right size so that, with the right strap adjustments, it conforms to your body regardless of the hiking clothes you happen to be wearing.

Make sure all your gear fits inside the pack. Tighten or loosen the straps inside and outside the pack that aren't involved with the pack's suspension—or how the pack "hangs" on the frame—to conform the soft body of the pack to its contents. Then, tighten or loosen the hip belt buckle and the stabilizer straps on the hip belt, the load adjusters at the tops of the shoulder straps, the shoulder strap adjusters at the bottom of the shoulder straps, and the sternum strap, to get the right fit. This way, your gear won't shift inside the pack and the pack won't shift on you when you move.

For fitting a backpack, start with the hip belt and make sure it rests comfortably on your hips. You should be able to tighten it enough over a T-shirt so that it holds the weight of the pack on your hips; you should also be able to buckle it over your thickest jacket. If the pack has a lumbar pad, it should rest against your lower back, above your butt. On a day pack and backpack, the shoulder straps should rest on top of your shoulders and stay put without engaging the sternum strap. The shoulder and sternum straps, engaged, should not rub against your neck or collarbone.

Try on several day packs or backpacks so you can feel the differences in fit. Walk around the store, sit down, and stand up. Swing your arms to see if they rub against the sides of your pack (they should not) and twist your body to see if the pack shifts (it should not). On a backpack, the majority of the pack's weight should be on your hips, and it should be snug enough to move with you but not so tight that it restricts your movement.

Do all of this and make sure you're happy with the fit, style, capacity, color, features, and price before you make your decision. You may be using this pack for many years and over many miles, so don't make a decision you'll regret. Your pack choice isn't as important as your choice of footwear, but it's a close second.

Packs and duffels come in a variety of sizes, capacities, and styles.

PACKING FOR YOUR ADVENTURE

Wear your hiking clothes to the trailhead so you can get a quick start. If you have a long drive or you're hiking in cold or inclement weather, dress comfortably for the drive—hiking shirt, pants, and sneakers or sandals—and pack the rest of your clothes in your duffel. Items like hiking socks and boots, jacket, hat, poles, and traction can go in the duffel. If you don't own a duffel bag, a plastic bin works fine. If you have food items like sandwiches or drinks that you'd like to keep cold, bring a small cooler for the drive.

At the trailhead, assess the temperature and weather conditions and decide which items to pull from your duffel and put them on right away. Stash the rest in your pack for later. Just make sure to check your duffel and cooler for items that need to go into your pack before you head off on your hike.

Packing for a Day Hike

First, pack your water and drinks. Fill your hydration bladder (reservoir) and water bottles or flasks. The bladder goes in the bladder pocket, if there is one, and the water and other drinks go in the bottom of the pack, evenly distributed on each side. If you are not using a bladder, put at least one bottle in an outside pocket of your pack for easy access.

Second, put in small, heavy items like your first-aid kit, fire starter, repair kit, and emergency shelter. You can pack all of these in one bag to keep them from getting mixed in with your clothes. That way, if you have to grab them fast, you can dig your hand into your pack and pull out the whole bag without having to locate the individual kits.

Third, add your food and clothing, with the heavier items on the bottom. Pack them around the water and other heavy items to keep them from shifting around in your pack. If there's a high chance of precipitation, put your rain jacket on top in the main compartment so you can get to it quickly. If not, it can go lower in the pack.

Fourth, put the items you'll be grabbing most often in outside compartments. Your toilet kit, sunscreen, lip balm, maps and directions plus a pen or pencil, snack bars, and trekking poles can go in these pockets and pouches. Pack your feminine urinary director (FUD) in a pocket on your hip belt or any pouch that you can get to without taking off your pack. (See chapter 8 for more information.) If you expect to be out past sunset, be mindful of where you store your headlamp and batteries so you're not fumbling for them in the dark.

Finally, if your pack has a key fob, use it. Otherwise, put your keys in a zippered compartment (preferably one that you won't be opening on your hike) or in a zippered pocket of your pants or jacket.

Packing for a Car Camp

For car camping, pack your day pack just like you would for a day hike. Everything else can go in bins or duffels. Think of this as packing four rooms: bedroom, bathroom, kitchen, and garage.

Your "bedroom" includes a tent; sleeping pad, cot, or air mattress with pump; sleeping bag; blankets; and pillow. You can also bring a small battery-powered light or fan to put in your tent. Also bring pajamas, an extra pair of socks, and sandals or insulated booties to wear around camp.

Your "bathroom" comprises your toilet and cleanup kits (discussed in chapter 8, "Personal Care"). You can use the ones from your day pack or create separate kits for camping, but if you have just one set, make sure you bring them into the tent with you at night and then put them back in your pack the next morning. If you plan to pee inside the tent at night instead of outdoors or in a toilet, bring a pee bottle or bladder and pack it with your bedroom items so it ends up inside the tent.

The "kitchen" includes a camp stove, fuel, coffeepot or French press, pots and pans, lighter, cooking utensils, an insulated mug for morning coffee or tea, plates, bowls, and eating utensils. Pack your food in bags, bins, or coolers, and don't forget condiments like salsa, ketchup, and mustard.

Finally, the "garage" includes gear beyond the essentials that you may need for the weather or terrain, such as trekking poles, snowshoes, an ice axe, and crampons.

For more on what to pack for car camping, check out chapter 5, "Camping and Cooking." Once you have everything you need for your trip, pack your bedroom in a duffel that you can throw inside your tent once it's set up, and load your kitchen into a plastic bin. Just like with your pack, empty your duffel and bins after your camping trip and replenish used or soiled items with new or clean ones.

Packing for a Backpacking Trip

Packing for a backpacking trip is like putting everything from your day pack *and* your car-camping containers into one big pack. Obviously, you won't fit all those items into a pack, so the key is to substitute smaller, lighter items made especially for backpacking. Just like with a day pack, load your backpack with the heavier items on the bottom, lighter items on top, and stuff that you want to get to quickly on the top of the main compartment, in the pack's lid, and in outside pockets and pouches.

First, stuff your sleeping bag into the main compartment. If you're using a hammock instead of a tent, stuff your underquilt in this section too. Next, put your tent and tent footprint or ground cloth, or your hammock, tarp, or bivy sack, in the main compartment of the pack, on top of your sleeping bag. Set the tent poles aside; those can go in a side pouch on the outside of your pack. If you're sharing a tent with other people, split up the parts of the tent so no one is carrying all the weight. If your sleeping pad isn't waterproof, you'll need to stuff that into your pack also, along with the pump.

Second, pack your water and drinks: the hydration bladder in the inside bladder pocket and bottles and flasks in the bottom, around the tent.

Third, put in other weighty items like your bear canister or bag, cooking kit, fuel, water filter, first-aid kit, fire starter, repair kit, and emergency shelter. You can pack all these inside one or two bags—cooking items in one and everything else in another—to keep them from getting lost in your clothes. If you plan to filter water along the way instead of at camp, keep the filter on top of your pack where you can get to it quickly.

Fourth, add your food and clothing, with the heavier items on the bottom. If you're carrying a bear canister, pack the food in it. If there's a high chance of precipitation, put your rain jacket on top in the main compartment so you can get to it quickly. You can also stick it into a "shovel pocket" if your pack has one. This is an open pocket on the front of your pack designed to carry a shovel, but it's more useful for stashing items like jackets, hats, and sunscreen.

Fifth, put anything you'll be grabbing most often in outside compartments. Your toilet and cleanup kits, sunscreen, lip balm, maps and directions plus a pen or pencil, and snack bars can fit into the lid of your pack and in pockets on the hip belt and shoulder straps. Headlamp and batteries can go into the zippered mesh pocket under the lid so you can get to them in the dark but also to avoid accidentally losing them when you're removing other items from the lid. Packing batteries inside this compartment also gives them an extra layer of fabric so they're not as exposed to the cold, which can drain them. If you carry a GPS, attach it to the outside of your pack where you can see it while you move. Some packs have a loop on the shoulder strap for this. If your pack does not, create one with nylon cord or a small locking carabiner.

Sixth, keys can go inside the pack lid's mesh compartment, on a key fob in your pack, or in another zipped compartment in your pack or your clothing. Some people prefer to keep their keys on them in case they lose their pack, while others prefer to keep them in their pack in case they accidentally leave a jacket (with keys in the pocket) behind.

Finally, the seventh step is to hang the bulky, waterproof items on the outside of your pack. Trekking poles go into a side pocket and tent poles go into the opposite side pocket. If your sleeping pad is waterproof, attach it to the bottom front of the pack with straps.

These are general packing guidelines; after a few outings you may discover your own packing preferences. Figure out what works for you and stick to it so you always know where everything is. That way, you can get to items quickly, and you can ask a hiking buddy to get to them for you so you don't have to drop your pack every time you need something.

Packing Extra Items for Mixed Terrain

Rock scrambling, rock climbing, ice climbing, and travel on ice or snow require gear you wouldn't carry on a typical hike or in your backpack. This gear is usually heavy and bulky, but most of it's waterproof, so you can strap it on the outside of your pack.

Anything attached to the outside should be close to the pack for the narrowest overall profile. This keeps the weight of your pack more centered over your hips and prevents gear from catching in tree branches or scraping against cliff faces. It should be firmly attached so it doesn't swing away from your pack when you move.

Store your helmet inside your pack, on top, if there's room. If there isn't, strap it to the middle front of the pack with straps and add small carabiners or nylon cord to hold it in place. Store all your other climbing gear—harness, shoes, protection, etc.—in the bottom of your pack. If you're carrying the rope, you can store it on top of your pack, in a separate rope bag, or carry it across your shoulders. Climbing gear is heavy, so split it up among your climbing buddies.

Ice tools can be strapped to the front of your pack. Some packs are specially made to carry them, so if you think you'll be doing a lot of ice climbing, consider getting a pack like this. Strap crampons and traction spikes to the outside of your pack or store them in a protective case and stick them inside your pack.

To attach an ice axe, locate the large loop on the bottom of your pack. Slide the length of the axe down through this loop, then flip it head down, spike end up, with the adze facing to the side and the pick turned in. Secure the handle with a side strap. Strap snowshoes to the outside of your pack with the pack straps; if necessary, add some webbing and carabiners to secure them tightly.

For traveling with avalanche gear, strap your beacon over your base layer and under your warmer layers to keep it off your skin but protected from the cold. Store the probe and snow shovel inside your pack to prevent them from being torn off if you're caught in an avalanche. If you plan to spend a lot of time in avalanche country, consider getting a pack specially outfitted for carrying these items.

Balance the weight so one side of your pack isn't heavier than the other. Pack your bag at home and wear it around the house or on a short local hike to see how it feels before you head out on a longer outing.

Ultralight Packing

Going *ultralight* refers to paring down your clothing and gear to the minimum weight while maintaining an acceptable level of safety and comfort. Women who want to move fast, who travel for long distances, or who just

In addition to day packs and backpacks, slim packs for rock climbing and vests for trail running are available for their respective activities.

Keep all your gear in one place for easy, convenient packing.
PHOTO BY SUSAN JOY PAUL

want to decrease the stress on their bodies created by carrying a heavier pack opt for ultralight gear and clothing. To go ultralight, look for a frameless pack or one with a removable frame. For some hikes, you can get by with a vest or fanny pack. Remove packaging, tags, and labels that add weight from your gear and clothing. Opt for ultralight sleeping and cooking systems and plan to treat water along your route instead of carrying it all with you. Ultralight travel is a big topic. If you wish to pursue it, get a book on the subject and see what works for you.

GEAR STORAGE

Keep your pack and gear in one place—a space in your closet or garage, or a gear room dedicated to your outdoor life. Make a list of everything you need to pack for a day hike, car camping, and backpacking and keep it with your gear so you can load up your car, cooler, duffel, and other containers quickly before an adventure. After every hike, empty your pack, dispose of trash, clean out your toilet and cleanup kits, wash your cooking and eating gear, replenish used items, and recharge batteries. Compression sacks make soft items smaller to fit in your pack, but be sure to unpack sleeping bags and clothing as soon as you can to prevent damage to the fibers. Air them out and wash regularly. Wash all your clothing after a hike so it has time to dry before your next hike.

As you acquire more gear, put together a system for storing it. Hanging gear racks, mesh bags, bins, and shelving combine to hold everything from maps to snowshoes and will keep you organized. Store everything out of direct sunlight, which can degrade fabrics, ropes, and other soft items.

TAKE STEPS

1. Gather your gear and clothing for a day hike, car camp, or backpack and figure out how much pack capacity you'll need.
2. Do some online window shopping to get an idea of current pack styles, features, and prices.
3. Get a friend to help measure you for a pack, then head to your local outdoor retailer and try some on.

Jean Aschenbrenner camps in Kilpacker Basin the night before a climb of Mount Wilson in the San Miguel Mountains near Telluride. PHOTO BY KEN NOLAN

CHAPTER 5

CAMPING AND COOKING

IF YOU CAMP OVERNIGHT, you will have to find a campsite, pitch your tent, and prepare meals. You'll also need to add a sleeping system and cooking system to your gear list. In this chapter, we'll discuss the different campsite and gear options for overnight trips.

CAMPING OUT

The kind of campsite you choose depends on how long you're going to be on the trail. For a one-day hike, you can camp at the trailhead or at a campground. Multiday hikes require camping off the trail or at an established backcountry campsite.

Trailhead and campground camping—*car camping*—doesn't mean "sleeping in your car." Instead, you pull into a parking spot at the trailhead, a campground, or at a pull-out on the side of the road (where it's allowed) and set up your tent. You still have access to your vehicle and can store your gear and food in it. If you arrive at the trailhead late at night or in inclement weather, you *can* actually skip the tent and sleep in your car (if there's enough room to lie down), and in really cold weather, you may prefer it.

With *backcountry camping*, also known as *dispersed camping*, you have no access to your car so you have to fit all your camping gear, cooking gear, and food in your backpack and carry it from trailhead to campsite—sometimes several campsites. Dispersed camping is legal on most public lands and by permit in wilderness areas.

If you have a long day hike planned and want to get an early start, instead of driving to the trailhead at the crack of dawn, consider heading to a campground or trailhead the night before to car-camp. Not all trailheads allow car camping, so find this out ahead of time. For a back-packing trip, identify the best trailside sites ahead of time if possible.

Before you buy any camping gear, think about where you're going to camp. You'll have to get a sleeping system—tent, sleeping bag, and pad—and a cooking kit. If you're going to be both car-camping and backcountry-camping, choose gear that works for backcountry camping. You can always add blankets, pillows, pots, and pans to a backcountry setup for car camping, but you can't stuff all your car-camping gear into a backpack.

Campground Camping

Car camping at a campground is easier for beginners and comes with conveniences you won't find in the backcountry. Each site has space for your tent and a parking spot for your car, and some have amenities like full bathrooms, laundry facilities, and showers. Campsites often include a picnic table, fire ring, and—in bear country—a bear locker to keep your food safe, with pit toilets and potable water nearby. Some sites have camp hosts who live on the premises during certain months, while others are self-serve sites. Campgrounds usually have tent pads—level gravel areas—so you don't have to locate a flat surface safe from the elements. Most sites come with a parking spot close to the tent pad, so you don't have to walk far with all your gear. Unlike backcountry camping, you don't have to fit your camping gear into your backpack or haul it for miles to a campsite. You can stash everything in your trunk, including a cooler full of food and drinks. If you're doing a day hike and you want to camp out before or after the hike, and trailhead or pull-out camping is not available or allowed, reserving a site at a campground makes sense. Having a reserved site gives you peace of mind, especially if you're driving a long way and don't want to risk arriving at your destination with no place to pitch your tent for the night.

The cons to campgrounds are that most of them charge a fee and that you forfeit the wilderness experience of backcountry camping. Many require a reservation, and during the busy summer season, popular campgrounds fill up weeks and even months in advance. Peace and privacy are not a given at campgrounds. Even though most have "quiet hours," not everyone abides by them. However, some campgrounds do offer peace and privacy, especially in the off-season. A campground is a good choice for your first camping experience, or if you don't have sleeping and cooking systems small enough to stuff into a pack.

To reserve a site, locate the campgrounds closest to your planned hike. Websites like recreation.gov and reserveamerica.com list campgrounds by location. Available sites and dates are labeled with an A, those that are reserved are labeled with an R, and W sites are walk-up sites, which are offered on a first come, first served basis. Don't confuse walk-up campground sites with walk-*in* sites. By contrast, walk-in sites typically provide a shared parking area and require a short walk from car to campsite, so you'll have to haul your tent and other gear more than a few yards to set up camp. Book the site for the nights you'll need, paying attention to check-in and check-out times.

When you book your site, look at the campground map on the website so you know where your site is and can locate it in the dark if you have to. Identify the nearest toilets so you can find those in the dark, too. Ideally, plan to arrive at camp at least one or two hours before sunset so you can set up in the light. Timeanddate.com or a weather app can give you sunset times, and from there—and taking into consideration driving time, traffic, and gas and bathroom stops—you can determine what time to leave your house to drive to the campground.

Before you leave for the trailhead in the morning, figure out if you'll be back in time to tear down camp before check-out. If you won't, unless you have a reservation for another night, you'll have to get up early enough to pack everything back into your car before heading to the trailhead.

Trailhead Camping

Trailhead camping is car camping without all the amenities of a campground. You basically park at the trailhead and set up your tent. Where it's allowed, trailhead camping is a convenient option that sets you up for an early start on the trail. Trailhead campsites usually don't require a reservation, and with no check-in or check-out times, you can show up as early as you like and you don't have to tear down your tent before hitting the trail.

The downside to trailheads is that there is no guarantee you will find a spot to park or set up your tent. Popular trailheads fill up early, especially on weekends. Some trailheads have toilets and potable water, but many do not. If you do get a spot, you could be awakened in the night by latecomers and early in the morning by hikers getting an early start on the trail. Many avid hikers prefer to avoid the reservation process, cost, and the early-morning drive from camp to trail associated with campgrounds, opting instead to accept the risks of trailhead camping.

Verify that camping is allowed at the trailhead by checking the respective land use office's website or calling the ranger district ahead of time. If you can't camp at the trailhead, ask if other free and legal primitive sites, such as roadside pull-outs, exist near the trailhead.

At the trailhead, find a flat spot big enough for your tent and with room to spare for cooking. Try not to set up too close to other campers if you can help it. At busy trailheads this isn't always possible, so just do the best you can. Be respectful of other campers, keeping the lights down and the noise to a minimum from dark to dawn.

Backcountry Camping

Backcountry camping is a great choice for the hiker who prefers solitude. In most places where backcountry camping is allowed, there is no fee to camp and reservations are not required. You choose where to set up your tent, when to set it up, and when to take it down. Backcountry camping is necessary for trips that take more than a day. It's also a good option for very long day hikes: You can hike up the trail a mile or so in the evening and set up camp, then on the second day, do your hike, tear down camp, and head back to the trailhead.

Backcountry camping is quite different from car camping mainly because you have to carry everything in your pack, including the tent, cooking supplies, and food. This means you'll need a bigger pack and camping and cooking gear small and light enough to fit inside it without weighing you down. Lighter gear is typically more expensive, too, so you may have to buy one piece at a time, or buddy up with someone who also wants to backcountry-camp so you can share gear.

Some areas have designated backcountry sites and require a reservation and charge a fee. These are typically public lands that are so popular, limiting the number of campers is necessary in order to maintain the pristine nature of the environment. In popular areas and wilderness areas, you may need to apply for a special permit, too, so again, contact the land use office for more information.

Unlike car camping where you set up your tent near your vehicle, with backcountry camping, you pick a site off the trail. Consider these factors before you drop your pack and pull out your tent:

> › When you plan your hike, look at the map and identify potential sites to pitch your tent. Consider how far you're likely to hike each

day and find locations near the end points that are best suited to tent camping.

> Try to locate a spot you can get to an hour or two before sunset so you don't have to set up your tent in the dark.

> Water is heavy, and you need a lot of it for hiking and cooking. You can either carry it all in (not ideal), filter water from lakes and streams along the way, or—the best solution—carry enough for the first day, and camp near natural sources where you can filter water every night.

> Camp at least 200 feet away from lakes and streams to avoid sullying the water, but not so far that you have to go on a long hike every time you need to get more water.

> Camp far enough away from the trail and other campsites so you don't infringe on other hikers' and campers' backcountry experience.

> Pick a flat area large enough to accommodate your tent with room around the perimeter for cooking, eating, and packing.

> Look for places where others have camped so you can reuse their spots instead of impacting another natural area.

> Avoid low areas that can flood. Wet spots attract bugs and increase condensation inside your tent.

> High areas can make good campsites because they're less likely to flood and the breezes keep bugs at bay. However, take into account the weather and avoid sites that are exposed to high winds or lightning strikes.

> Look around for hazards like fallen debris. Don't put yourself in the path of overnight rockslides or avalanches. Never camp near the top of a cliff—you could step off the edge in the night— or at the bottom of one, where you could get hit by falling rocks.

> Camping under trees offers shade and protects your tent from precipitation and wind. However, do not camp under dead trees, beetle-kill trees, or trees with soft wood prone to breakage. If a tree looks dead or there are a lot of dead branches on the ground, find another spot.

> Look for nearby, healthy trees to hang your food off the ground and out of reach of animals. Again, avoid dead trees, and never hang anything on one.

> Look for a site with nearby boulders and tree stumps to sit on.

Setting Up Camp

Once you have a campsite, remove any loose rocks and branches from the tent pad or area where you're setting up the tent. Lay out the tent footprint and set up the tent according to the directions. A footprint keeps the bottom of the tent clean and dry, but you can substitute a tarp or even a lawn-size garbage bag split lengthwise.

TENTS

Tents come in three-season and four-season varieties. Other than the most ultralight styles, all tents have a main compartment made of fabric and mesh that's held up by telescoping tent poles and anchored to the ground with tent stakes. Most tents are double-walled, with a waterproof rainfly (or *fly*) that covers the tent, keeping rain, wind, and debris from entering the mesh panels but allowing for air circulation around the main body of the tent. The tent is secured to the ground with stakes. Use a rock to pound the stakes into the ground, and for car camping, pack a hammer. The fly rests on top and is anchored to the tent with fasteners. Most tents have *guy lines*—cords that secure the fly to the ground and are useful in wet or windy weather. Guy lines pull the fly taut, away from the tent body so rainwater won't seep in, and they provide more structure and security to the tent so it's less likely to collapse or fly away in high winds. They're not necessary in most conditions, but if you do use them, remember where they are so you don't trip over them in the dark.

Before you shop for a tent, think about the seasons when you'll be camping, temperatures and weather conditions, whether you'll be by yourself in the tent or sharing it with others, how much money you want to spend, and for backpacking, how much space the tent will take up in your pack and how much weight you want to carry.

Seasonal tents

A three-season tent can be used most of the year but isn't suitable for winter camping or anytime the temperatures dip below freezing. Four-season tents are sturdier and made of thicker fabric to withstand the cold and wind, with fewer, smaller mesh panels and a large vestibule where you can cook meals. They're also heavier, so if you don't expect to be camping in cold weather, a three-season tent is a lighter, less expensive choice.

Tent size, weight, and capacity

Tents come in many sizes, from minimalist, ultralight, single-wall solo tents to huge cabin tents that you can literally walk around in. For backpacking, a one-, two-, or three-person tent is all you'll need—or want to carry. A one-person tent will save you on cost and weight but typically has just enough room for your sleeping pad and bag, and not much else. If you're backpacking over several nights, you might prefer a two-person tent with more room. If you're hiking with others, consider going with a larger, shared tent and split up the parts to share the weight. Before you buy a tent, make sure it fits in your pack.

For car camping, weight and size are less of a concern because you're hauling your tent only from the car to a nearby campsite. Still, think about how much space you'll have to set it up at the campground or trailhead and how much space you really need inside the tent.

Other tent features

When shopping for a tent, check out all the features, such as mesh panels, doors, and vestibules. Mesh lets in more air—nice for hot summer nights—and allows for more circulation and less condensation on cold nights. Tent doors may be located at the foot or on the side. Some open on two sides—nice if you're sharing a tent and don't want to crawl over other people to get in and out. Two doors also add weight, because of the extra zipper and closures. A tent vestibule is an extension of the fly over the door of the tent. This keeps rain from getting in through the door and provides a space to store hiking boots and other dirty items you may not want in the tent. You can also cook in the vestibule *if* it's properly ventilated for cooking. Never cook in a tent or vestibule that isn't made for cooking; the stove's fumes could literally kill you.

To get an idea of how much room you'll have inside, look at the height of the tent and the slope of the "walls." Some sides are low or sloped, and you can't sit upright, while others have more vertical walls and offer more headroom. Check the specifications of the tent on the manufacturer's site for details. If your local retailer has the tent set up in their store, get inside and see how it fits.

Some women prefer bright- or light-colored tents that let in a lot of sunlight. This makes it easier to see inside the tent during daylight hours and easier to get cleaned up and dressed before a hike. Blackout tents shut out the light, even during full daylight, which is great if you have an early start and need to get to bed before the sun sets. Tents have interior compartments on the sides for stashing items you might need during the night, overhead gear lofts to store things off the floor so they don't get lost in the bedding, and hooks to hang things like candles and fans. Every additional feature adds both convenience and weight.

Tent setup

Practice setting up your tent at home before you leave for an adventure. The instructions are printed on a tag attached to the tent or the tent bag it's stored in, but after a long day on the trail, you'll want to be able to set up camp fast without reading fine print or looking at diagrams.

To set up your tent in the wild, locate a flat, dry area 200 feet or more from the trail and water sources and lay out the footprint. Think about which way you want the door of the tent to face. You can face it toward a clearing where you'll be cooking, or toward the east to catch the morning sun, or perpendicular to the wind's direction, to prevent dirt and debris from flying in through the open door. Lay the body of the tent on the footprint, top side up, with the door where you want it. Extend the telescoping poles and slip them through the tent sleeves or plastic hooks according to the diagram and fasten them into the grommets at the base of the tent body. Move the tent to center it over the footprint, pull the poles outward to remove any slack in the tent body, and stake the tent to the ground. Tap the stakes in with a rock or hammer. Slip the fly on top, attach it to the tent, and if it's windy or wet, use the guy lines to stake it out.

Put your sleeping pad, sleeping bag, and a pillow (if you have one) in the tent, along with your pack. Before you bed down for the night, stash items you'll need to get to after dark in the side pockets or gear lofts. This includes items like a headlamp and toilet kit. Keep electronics near or inside your sleeping bag to prevent the batteries from being depleted. In cold temps, store fuel in the bottom of your sleeping bag to prevent it from becoming too cold and unusable. Boots, booties, and sandals can go at the bottom of the tent or under a vestibule. Keep a liter of water handy for nighttime drinks.

Remove anything that smells from your pack and tent and stash it in a bear-proof container. This includes food, snacks, toothpaste, and other scented items that can attract animals.

Tent takedown

The inside of your tent may be damp in the morning from condensation and wet on the outside from dew, rain, or frost. Ideally, let it dry before you repack it. Shake off the excess moisture and move it to a sunny spot to dry while you cook breakfast. If you're returning to the same campsite later in the day, you can leave it up to dry.

SLEEPING BAGS

Sleeping bags come in different sizes, weights, shapes, and "warmths," or temperature ratings. Like all your camping gear, think about where you're going to use it before you buy. For backpacking, choose one that's small and light enough for your pack. If you'll be using the bag in all seasons, choose one that will keep you warm on the coldest nights. If your bag's too warm, you can wear fewer clothes, unzip the bag, or just sleep under or on top of it, but if it isn't warm enough, you will be cold no matter what.

Make sure your bag's big enough to accommodate you from head to foot. A snug mummy-shaped bag has less air space, will keep you warmer, and may weigh less. A rectangular bag gives you more room to move around, and you can store hiking clothes, batteries, electronics, and fuel in the bottom on cold nights. If the retailer allows it, slip into the bag before you buy it. Try it on for size and comfort.

Bags are insulated with natural or synthetic materials. You can add more warmth and comfort with a bag liner and a pillow; while they add more weight to your pack, your improved sleep may make the extra ounces worth it.

A tent, sleeping pad, and sleeping bag keep you warm and dry overnight on the trail.

Unpack and air out all of your bedding after every hike. Wash the liner, if you have one. Wash the bag at least once every season, following the manufacturer's instructions. If your sleeping bag came with a big cotton sack for storage, use it. Otherwise, store it loosely in a large pillowcase. Leave it uncompressed so you don't crush the fill, which impacts the insulating properties.

SLEEPING PADS
Inflatable and closed-cell foam sleeping pads provide a cushion and insulate your body from the hard, cold ground. Foam pads are thin, light, and waterproof, and they can be attached to the outside of a pack, making them a good choice for backpacking. However, they usually don't provide as much cushion or insulation as inflatable pads. Most inflatable pads contain an insulating fill. A pad that is not filled may become very cold overnight, as the air inside cools to the temperature of the ground. For backcountry camping, look for a self-inflating pad or one that comes with a lightweight hand pump. For car camping, you can use a bigger hand or foot pump, or even a battery-powered pump.

Pad insulation is rated by R-value, with a higher R-value denoting more insulation. However, these values are not standardized between manufacturers: One company's R-value 1 may be another company's R-value 3. Before you buy, find out the temperature range the R-value is recommended for. Also consider your personal needs and preferences. Some people get cold easily and need more insulation while others sleep better when they're slightly cool. Try out the pad before you buy it. Lie on your back and your side. Ideally, your back and hips should be comfortable enough that you'll be able to sleep. Like sleeping bags, pads should be aired out after every hike and stored uncompressed.

Cots, Tarps, Hammocks, and Bivy Tents and Sacks

Most women camp with the traditional tent, bag, and pad setup, but you have other options. For more cushioning on a car camp, a canvas cot adds space between you and the ground. For lighter travel, you can sleep inside a bivouac shelter, tent or *bivy sack*, or under a tarp. Check the weather to make sure you'll be warm and dry enough. In recent years, hammock camping has gained in popularity, so that's another option if there are trees at your campsite. Depending on humidity and overnight temperatures, you may want to add an underquilt, top quilt, and mosquito netting for more comfort and a better night's sleep.

ADVICE TO INTERNATIONAL PASSENGERS ON CARRIER LIABILITY

Passengers on a journey involving an ultimate destination or a stop in a country other than the country of departure are advised that international treaties known as the Montreal Convention, or its predecessor, the Warsaw Convention, including its amendments, may apply to the entire journey, including any portion thereof within a country. For such passengers, the treaty, including special contracts of carriage embodied in applicable tariffs, governs and may limit the liability of the carrier in respect of death of or injury to passengers, and for the destruction or loss of, or damage to, baggage, and for the delay of passengers and baggage. For additional information on international baggage liability limitations, including domestic portions of international journeys, see AA.com.

NOTICE OF INCORPORATED TERMS OF CONTRACT

Air Transportation, whether it is domestic or international (including domestic portions of international journeys), is subject to the individual terms of the transporting air carriers, which are herein incorporated by reference and made part of the contract of carriage. Other carriers on which you may be ticketed may have different conditions of carriage. International air transportation, including the carrier's liability, may also be governed by applicable tariffs on file with the U.S. and other governments and by the Warsaw Convention, as amended, or by the Montreal Convention. Incorporated terms may include, but are not restricted to: 1. Rules and limits on liability for personal injury or death, 2. Rules and limits on liability for baggage, including fragile or perishable goods, and availability of excess valuation charges, 3. Claim restrictions, including time periods in which passengers must file a claim or bring an action against the air carrier, 4. Rights on reconfirmation of reservations, check-in times and refusal to carry, 6. Rights of the air carrier and limits on liability for delay or failure to perform service, including schedule changes, substitution of alternate air carriers or aircraft and rerouting.

You can obtain additional information on items 1 through 6 above at any U.S. location where the transporting air carrier's tickets are sold. You have the right to inspect the full text of each transporting air carrier's terms at its airport and city ticket offices. You also have the right, upon request, to receive (free of charge) the full text of the applicable terms incorporated by reference from each of the transporting air carriers. Information on ordering the full text of each air carrier's terms is available at any U.S. location where the air carrier's tickets are sold. Additionally, American Airlines' contract terms are found on AA.com under the "Legal" link. You can reach American Airlines on the web, using the following link: www.aa.com/customerrelations.

REV. 3/11

PASSENGER TICKET AND BAGGAGE CHECK
SUBJECT TO CONDITIONS OF CONTRACT
AMERICAN AIRLINES

ISSUED BY

NAME OF PASSENGER (NOT TRANSFERABLE)
ROBINETTE/KIMBERLYA
X/O FROM MADISON
X/O CHICAGO OHARE

ENDORSEMENTS/RESTRICTIONS ***************
* * *
* * *
* * *
* *
* ***************

ORIGINAL ISSUE

FARE CALCULATION

FARE

TAXFEE/CHARGE
TAX/FEE/*STATE
TAX/FEE/ *US
TOTAL *******

21AUG21   MADISON
ISS. AGENT /₁/MSN
0CS   CARR   FLIGHT   CLASS DATE   TIME
             AA 3677 V 21AUG940A   FARE BASIS

BOARDING PASS ISSUED IN EXCHANGE FOR
BOARDING ENDS 15 MINUTES
BEFORE DEPARTURE

PRIORITY

EQUIV. FARE PAID   FORM OF PAYMENT

00128858342936

STOCK CONTROL NUMBER TX

PLACE OF ISSUE
FCI
TOUR CODE
STATUS NOT VALID BEFORE—NOT VALID AFTER

PNR CODE
CLGIRQ /AA   CONJ. TKT. NO.

GROUP 1
SEAT 10B

PNR CODE

COUPON   AIRLINE   SEQ. NO. ALLOW *PCS *CK.WT. *UNCK.WT. CK

3 001 7633328419 2

REV. 2/11 CPN113922
PRINTED IN U.S.A. BY MAGNETIC TICKET AND LABEL CORP., DALLAS, TX

AMERICAN AIRLINES
BOARDING PASS

NAME OF PASSENGER
ROBINETTE/KIMBERLYA

X/O FROM MADISON
X/O CHICAGO OHARE
AMERICAN EAGLE

CARRIER FLIGHT CLASS DATE TIME   PLACE OF ISSUE
AA 3677 V 21AUG940A
REVALIDATION   STATUS NOT VALID BEFORE—NOT VALID AFTER

SEAT 10B   SMOKE NO

BOARDING TIME   SEC. GROUP 1
910A

GATE
12

ADDITIONAL SEAT INFORMATION
PCS. CK. WT. UNCK. WT.   CK. WT.

BAGGAGE ID NR.   FORM SERIAL NO.

COUPON AIRLINE
0CS /MSN

one world
US

A lightweight bivy tent saves weight and space in your pack for long hauls. Lisa and Tim Heckel set up this cozy site on Segment 2 of the 500-mile-long Colorado Trail. Pikes Peak appears on the distant horizon. PHOTO BY TIMOTHY HECKEL

On warm, dry nights, you can even skip the tent and lay your pad and bag on the ground. If you have a truck and are camping at a trailhead, lay out your pad and bag in the truck bed. Waking up to open air and sunrise is an experience you won't forget.

COOKING OUT

Camp food preparation can be as simple or as complicated as you want to make it. Some women survive on fresh fruit and vegetables, protein bars, jerky, and trail mix. That's fine for day hikes, but when you're camping out, a hot meal makes a welcome start and end to a long day. The simplest camp meals require just boiling water. You'll need a stove, fuel, something to light the fire, and a pot to boil water in.

Stoves

Camping stoves vary in size, weight, surface type or platform, and the fuel they use. If you're only going to be car camping, any kind of camp stove works. Backcountry camping requires a stove that fits in your pack. If you're buying only one stove and you plan to do multiday hikes, make it a backcountry stove.

BACKCOUNTRY STOVES

Backcountry stoves come in three varieties: canister, integrated canister, and liquid fuel. *Canister stoves* are small, metal fixtures that screw into a canister-style fuel source and provide a platform for your pot. Some have built-in igniters, so you don't need a lighter to get them going. They're the lightest stoves available and ideal for backpacking. Isobutane gas canisters are readily available at outdoor retailers and even some grocery stores, so finding fuel for your canister stove usually isn't a problem. However, they typically don't heat water as fast as other types of stoves, and the fuel canisters may not be available internationally. In extremely cold temperatures, canister stoves don't perform as well as other types. For winter camping, you'll want to keep the fuel in a warm place overnight so that it will work in the morning, or to be on the safe side, just opt for another type of stove. Still, these tiny stoves are a favorite under most conditions for their cost, size, and weight.

Integrated canister stoves combine a stove and a large cooking mug with a handle. They're heavier than simple canister stoves, but since you don't have to carry a separate pot, the trade-off may be worth it. Integrated canisters tend to heat water faster and some have wind screens around the flame. Some have simmer control. For instant meals, the simmer control doesn't matter, but if you need to cook something in the pot for a while, you need to control the flame. Like regular canister stoves, integrated stoves use isobutane fuel, which is easy to find on the road. However, in extreme cold, this fuel may not perform well, or at all.

Unlike canister stoves that sit on top of the fuel canister, *liquid fuel stoves* have their own base that sits on the ground to provide a platform for your pot. They heat water fast and perform well in extreme cold. Liquid fuel is cheaper and easier to find internationally. Liquid fuel stoves are heavier than canister styles and are kind of overkill for the average outdoor adventure, but they're the go-to choice for multiday mountaineering trips in cold weather and at high altitudes.

CAR-CAMPING STOVES

Since you're not limited by weight and size for car camping, you may want to consider a double-burner portable butane gas stove. This lets you cook in two pots or pans at once so you can boil water for coffee and oatmeal on one side while you make breakfast burritos on the other. Portable gas grills are another option. Think about the kinds of foods you want to eat and buy the right stove for the job.

OTHER STOVE OPTIONS

Wood, solid fuel, and alcohol stoves are other suitable options. They're just not as popular, and you may not always be able to locate fuel for them.

Pots and Pans

An integrated canister stove or a large pot for other stoves should hold enough water for a freeze-dried or dehydrated dinner with a little left over for cleanup. Most meals require about 2 cups of water, and even though they claim to feed two, you may want to eat the whole thing yourself. For solo cooking, get a 500- to 700-milliliter pot. If you're sharing gear and cooking for a friend, a 900- to 1,200-milliliter pot allows you to

Backcountry coffee mills, liquid fuel stoves, integrated canister stoves, and lightweight cooking and eating utensils are among the many backcountry cooking options.

boil enough water for both people. Pots are made from stainless steel, aluminum, and titanium. Stainless pots are very sturdy but heavier than aluminum and titanium, while titanium pots are lightest but cost more. Buy what you can afford, and make sure it has a tight-fitting lid and a handle. Items like backcountry coffeemakers and frying pans give you more cooking options, but you also will have to carry them and clean them. If you're car-camping, you can go all out with pots, frying pans, a French press or coffeepot, and anything else your appetite desires.

Cooking and Eating Utensils

Many meals come in self-contained pouches or cartons; you pour in cold or hot water to rehydrate the food. For these, a lightweight spoon and fork or a combination spork are all you need. If your meals aren't in waterproof pouches, get a large mug or bowl. Add an insulated mug or flask for coffee, tea, soup, and other foods that aren't packaged in a cooking pouch.

For trailhead and campground camping, your home pots, pans, plates, bowls, mugs, and utensils are fine to use. And if your site has a picnic table, you can even add a tablecloth, napkins, and candles.

Storing and Cooking Food and Cleanup

For car camping, whenever you're sleeping or away from your site, store all food in a bear-proof container in your trunk. Bears will break into cars to get to any food they see, and they know that coolers contain food. If you're camping on the trail, store your food in a bear-proof bag or canister and hang it between trees high enough off the ground so animals can't get to it. On some public lands, you're required to carry all your food in a bear-proof canister. These are heavy, but if it's required, get one. Campgrounds with bear activity usually have bear lockers—metal boxes with latches near your campsite. Never store food in the tent, which can attract animals; likewise, for smelly toiletries. Store it all in the bear locker, bag, or canister.

Once you have your tent set up, prepare your water. Chapter 6 details the options for preparing water to make it safe for cooking and drinking. If you're car-camping, just bring a gallon or two per person, per day— enough to cook all your meals and fill your water bottles or bladder. On the trail, prepare water at camp while it's still light out—enough for dinner, breakfast the next morning, and the next day's hike. That way, you won't have to do it in the morning when you're hungry and eager to hit the trail. After your meals, clean any dirty dishes and utensils with a little hot water and discard the water away from natural water sources and plants, and preferably on rocks or on the ground.

TAKE STEPS

1. Choose an area you'd like to explore and start planning an overnight stay.
2. Get the right camping and cooking gear, food, and fuel for your overnight camp.
3. Book a campsite or find a legal backcountry site. Pack for your campout and go.

Nutrition, hydration, and exercise pay off with healthy dividends for the woman in the wild. Jennifer Roach celebrates her sixty-seventh birthday with a summit hike to Vanderbilt Peak, New Mexico, with her dog, Izzi. PHOTO BY GERRY ROACH

YOU IN THE WILD

Bethany Burnett and a friend filter water at Lower Sand Creek Lake below Tijeras Peak in southern Colorado. PHOTO BY OTINA FOX

CHAPTER 6

WATER AND HYDRATION

WATER AND OTHER LIQUIDS are vital for quenching your thirst and keeping you hydrated. In the backcountry, women require more than the standard eight glasses per day. Heat, exercise, sweating, altitude, and frequent urination cause your body to use and release more water, and you need to make up for it.

WHAT SHOULD I DRINK?

Most of your hydration should come from water, but there are good reasons to add other drinks to the mix. When your body uses and releases water, it expels diluted minerals called *electrolytes* that you need to survive. You can easily replenish them with healthy food and beverages. Sports drinks like Gatorade and natural drinks like coconut water, V8 juice, and other fruit and vegetable waters, juices, and broths contain minerals like bicarbonate, calcium, chloride, magnesium, phosphate, potassium, and sodium.

Another reason to carry sweet and savory beverages is that you are more likely to drink if you have something tasty to break up the monotony of plain water. Add even more variety by choosing hot or cold drinks, depending on the season. In summer, cold drinks are refreshing. In winter, hot drinks such as cocoa, bouillon, and tea warm you from the inside. Insulated flasks keep cold drinks cold and hot drinks hot for many hours. Having a delicious beverage to look forward to can motivate you to keep moving until that next trail break. Fruits like oranges and apples contain water, too, and make a tasty treat. If you run out of water on a hike, having a juicy piece of fruit in your pack to munch on can be a lifesaver.

Some people enjoy energy drinks on the trail, but you're better off choosing healthier options. The effects of energy drinks are short-term and the quick rush you get from the caffeine and simple carbohydrates

Water bottles and insulated flasks are handy for carrying beverages on the trail.

may be followed by a rapid decrease in energy, or "crash." An occasional boost like a cup of coffee at breakfast or an energy block or gel on the trail is fine, but don't rely on caffeinated, sugary drinks, gels, blocks, or bars to keep you moving, as these are not sustainable energy sources.

Finally, avoid alcohol, which can lead to dehydration, headaches, nausea, and hangovers. If you want to celebrate an adventure with an alcoholic beverage, wait until you're somewhere safe—ideally, back at home. If you do partake in a post-hike beer or glass of wine, drink plenty of water to offset the dehydrating effects.

HOW MUCH WATER IS RIGHT FOR ME?

How much water your body needs depends on your weight, metabolism, activity, outside temperatures, and other factors, so there's no one-size-fits-all equation for figuring it out. Until you know how much you need, carry half a liter of liquids for every hour on the trail in moderate temperatures, on an easy to moderate hike. If you're in high heat and the hike is strenuous, carry 1 liter or more per hour. The other drinks should make up one-quarter to one-half of your total liquids. If you have a lot of water left when you get back to the trailhead, you either don't need that much water or you didn't drink enough. If you drink it all before you get back to

JENNIFER ROACH began hiking in August 1980 when her brother-in-law, Alan, took her up Scotland's iconic Ben Lomond. The next year she went up Colorado 14er Grays Peak. Her hiking partner Bill recommended she join the Colorado Mountain Club and she did, where she trained, made friends, and discovered new places to hike and climb. Jennifer summited all of Colorado's 14ers and 13ers, plus many other mountains. In 1998 she married adventurer and author Gerry Roach and together, they climbed around the American West and overseas. Jennifer pursued ultrarunning and endurance hiking, competing in races up to 100 miles long. In 2014, she and a friend, Susan, hiked the entire Colorado Trail. In 2017, 2018, and 2019, she hiked the Continental Divide Trail (CDT) through Colorado, New Mexico, and Wyoming, respectively. Jennifer still gets into the mountains with Gerry and their black mutt, Izzi, favoring the less popular, obscure peaks. She expects to hike the CDT through Montana to the Canadian border. Jennifer says, "Mark my words: I *will* reach that border someday, because I'm no quitter." To women aspiring to climb a mountain, Jennifer offers this advice: "Persevere. What feels difficult at first gets a little easier and more familiar each time you go out. Keep chugging along. Keep ascending. Keep your eyes on the prize. Focus on that summit. Above all, don't be a quitter."

the trailhead, bring more on your next outing. After a few trips, you'll have a good idea of how much to bring.

If you're not sure if you're drinking enough water, pay attention to your urine. On the trail, you should be taking pee breaks; if you're not, you may be dehydrated. Back at home, look in the toilet after your first pee. The water should look like lemonade—not iced tea.

HYDRATING BEFORE, DURING, AND AFTER YOUR ADVENTURES

Instead of waiting until the day of your hike to hydrate, drink plenty of water daily and especially the day before your hike. An easy way to get your daily water requirement is to fill a half-gallon jug first thing in the morning and make sure you finish it off by the end of the day. Another method is to keep a ten-ounce tumbler handy and chug the whole thing as soon as you wake up and again before you shower, before breakfast, lunch, and dinner, and finally, before you go to bed. That will give you sixty ounces of water plus whatever you get from other drinks.

When you pack, add drinks for the drive to the trailhead and for after your hike. Some drinks are made especially for pre- and post-exercise, which are fine but can be expensive. Boxed drinks like coconut water and chocolate milk (including nondairy options such as soy and nut milks) are inexpensive thirst-quenchers that taste great and are packed with carbohydrates and electrolytes to fuel your body pre-hike and help it recover post-hike.

PACKING WATER

When the temperatures are above freezing, use a portable hydration pack to carry water. A 3-liter bladder is large enough for most hikes. Fill the reservoir, tuck it into your pack, and feed the tube through the pack's hydration tube hole and the loops in the shoulder strap so the mouth-piece sits near your face, below your mouth. It should be out of the way but within easy reach so you can sip from it while you hike. When temperatures dip, water in the hydration pack's tubing can freeze. While you can sometimes clear the ice by blowing into the mouthpiece, it's best to leave the bladder at home on wintry days in favor of carrying drinks in insulated bottles and flasks.

Drain and clean hydration bladders and drink containers after every hike and allow them to dry. Bottles and flasks can go in the dishwasher, but hydration bladders require extra care. Clean them more thoroughly at least once every season with tablets made especially for cleaning bladders, or just use hot water and a couple teaspoons of baking soda and bleach. Add the solution, close the reservoir, and shake to mix. Squeeze the mouthpiece to allow a little solution to pass through it, then let the bladder sit for half an hour. Empty it, rinse it, give it another light wash with warm water and a bit of dishwashing liquid, then rinse again. If the tube is cloudy, remove the mouthpiece and pull a piece of cord through the tubing. Rinse everything again, stuff the reservoir with a few paper towels or a small cloth towel, and hang it up to dry. Replace worn mouthpieces and consider carrying an extra one in your repair kit in case you lose one during a hike.

Water weighs more than 2 pounds per liter and may be the heaviest item in your pack. For a day hike, bring enough water for the day. If you're doing a multiday hike, locate water sources like streams and lakes along your route. At camp, collect and prepare enough water for the evening meal, breakfast, and for the next day's hike so you don't have to do it in the morning. For long backpacks where you're carrying a heavy pack, instead of carrying all your water all day, start off with 1 or 2 liters and then stop to filter or sterilize a fresh liter as you need it. You can do this only if your route passes lakes or follows streams, so know the route and plan accordingly. This method adds time to your hike, but the lighter pack may be worth the extra time. And make sure that even if you start with just 1 liter, you're carrying enough empty containers to fill for meals and days when you won't have ready access to water sources.

Bladders or reservoirs, bottles, and cleaning kits help to ensure plenty of clean water for your hikes.

TREATING WATER FROM
NATURAL SOURCES

Tap water, bottled water, and water from potable taps is safe for drinking. But any water you gather from natural sources like lakes, streams, and snow must be treated to remove sediment or kill bacteria, parasites, and viruses. Boiling, filtering, purifying, and chemical sterilization make water safe for consumption. With any water treatment process, make sure no untreated water comes in contact with the rim of your water bottles so you don't accidentally ingest those stray, potentially contaminated droplets.

Water filters are a good choice because they allow you to pump a lot of water quickly, directly from a stream into your hydration bladder and bottles. At the campsite, decide whether to set up your tent or filter water first. If dark is quickly approaching, it might make more sense to drop your pack, get out all your water-filtering supplies, and head to the nearest source to collect water while it's still light out. In the dark, it's easier to set up a tent than it is to sit on a slippery riverbank filtering water. If you're hiking with other people, work together to get this chore done quickly or split up the work, with some people setting up camp while others go for water for everyone.

Read the instructions and prepare the filter in your sink at home before taking it on the trail. During use, part of the filter comes in contact with unfiltered water, so cleaning your filter is an important task. Drain and clean it properly after every hike.

In winter when water sources are frozen, collect snow in plastic bags or water bottles and boil it. Your drinking-water "snow patch"—where you collect snow for drinking and cooking water—should be on the opposite side of camp from your potty "snow patch," so you're not melting snow that someone peed in. Put a few drops of water in the bottom of the pan first to prevent scorching it, turn on your stove, and add snow a little at a time to melt. If the natural water sources are frozen but there's no snow on the ground, you may have to carry more water from the trailhead or locate a place where the water is moving or dripping, like an overhang or frozen waterfall. Overhanging ice can collapse, so use extreme caution if you gather water this way.

Finally, portable "pens" that use UV light from the sun for purification are a convenient choice for treating water on the go. They are less useful for treating large quantities of water. As with all water treatment products, follow the instructions carefully.

Filters, UV light pens, and chemicals make water safe for drinking.

Have a backup plan in case your water purification system breaks down or you lose it. Pack some chemical treatment tablets like chlorine dioxide or iodine in your first-aid kit for emergencies. Before giving chemically treated water to anyone in your group, make sure they're not allergic to the iodine or other ingredients found in these treatments. Unlike filtered or boiled water, chemically treated water requires a wait time before it's safe to drink. Follow the directions and make sure you wait long enough for the chemicals to take effect. Likewise, electro-chlorinators also require a waiting period. Read and follow the instructions. If they aren't printed on the product, cut them from the packaging and store them in your first-aid kit or water treatment kit. Water filtering and purifying methods vary in their ability to remove sediment and kill dangerous parasites, bacteria, and viruses. Ensure that yours does what you need it to do.

TAKE STEPS

1. Figure out how much water and other drinks to carry on your next hike.
2. Check out all the options for carrying and treating water and decide what you need right now and what you might want to purchase in the future.
3. Once you buy a water purification system, read the directions and test it at home. Then figure out where it fits best in your pack.

Nutrition is especially important for a clear head on difficult terrain. This photo captures the author descending the exposed upper pitches of Mount Wilson.

PHOTO BY DOUG HATFIELD

CHAPTER 7

FOOD AND NUTRITION

A NUTRITIOUS DIET gives your body what it needs to move and to recover. You need the right balance of carbohydrates, protein, and fats, plus fiber, vitamins, and minerals. If you're already active and eating healthy, you're ahead of the game, but if you're used to a sedentary lifestyle and unbalanced diet, expect to add nutrient-rich foods to fuel your outdoor adventures. The guidance in this chapter is intentionally general and meant to be considered along with what you know about your own body. Nutritional needs differ based on genetics and other factors, as do preferences. One woman may thrive on a paleo diet, while another performs better on a keto diet, and another follows a vegan diet for health and ethical reasons. Follow the basic rules of nutrition and tweak them to work for you.

WHAT TO EAT

What and how much you eat before, during, and after your hikes affects your performance and how quickly you recover. Since backcountry travel isn't always steady and consistent, you'll need enough energy not only to sustain you but also to provide some extra to pull from when the going gets tough, like pushing uphill, scrambling over rocks, and moving through other demanding terrain.

Eat Before You Hike

Your main source of energy before a hike should be complex carbohydrates. For day hikes and multiday treks, have a carb-rich meal the day before you hit the trail. Dinner should include a combination of whole grains, legumes, and vegetables. On the day of your hike, have a good breakfast with another healthy dose of carbohydrates. A mix of whole grains, fruits, nuts, and seeds provides complex carbs plus vitamins, minerals, protein, fats, and fiber. If you have a long drive to the trailhead, bring snacks in the car so you don't start your hike feeling hungry.

Recommended foods for pre-hike meals include the following:

Whole grains: Brown rice, soba noodles, whole-grain pasta, quinoa, oatmeal, buckwheat pancakes, whole-grain toast, and popcorn.

Legumes: Kidney beans, chickpeas (garbanzo beans), black beans, and lentils.

Fruits: Fresh or dried bananas, apples, oranges, grapefruit, blueberries, dates, raisins, and goji berries. Dried fruits also aid with digestion, so if you're prone to constipation, add a box of raisins to your pack and drink plenty of water to rehydrate them in your stomach.

Vegetables: Sweet potatoes, beets, peas, and corn.

Nuts and seeds: Almonds, walnuts, cashews, pistachios, pine nuts, peanut butter, almond butter, flaxseeds, chia seeds, sunflower seeds, and pumpkin seeds. Nuts and seeds are packed with nutrients, but they're typically high in calories, too. Add them to your diet but pay attention to portion sizes. Choose raw or dry roasted nuts and seeds instead of those that have been roasted in potentially unhealthy oils and at high temperatures, which can deplete them of their nutrients.

Leafy greens: Spinach, kale, broccoli, romaine lettuce, and bok choy are low in carbohydrates, but they add nutrients you may not be able to get from high-carb foods. Make sure to include them in your diet as well.

Fats: Don't remove fats from your diet, which are necessary for the absorption of nutrients in the foods you eat. Choose healthy fats from natural sources like avocados, dark chocolate, nuts, seeds, coconuts, and for cooking, extra virgin olive oil. Fats should be consumed daily, and in moderation.

Supplements: Take a multivitamin and mineral supplement every day to make up for nutritional gaps in your diet.

Don't wait until it's time to pack to think about nutrition. Put nutritious foods and drinks on your shopping list and make a place for them in your refrigerator and pantry.

Eat on the Trail

While fueling up before the hike is important, it won't sustain you. Eating at regular intervals during your hike is what will keep you going. We've all heard the saying "Eat when you're hungry." This doesn't apply on the trail because exercise can suppress your appetite, and hiking at high altitudes only increases this effect. Adding the physical, mental, and emotional pressures of staying "on schedule," getting in and out before dark, and various other factors can make some women reluctant to stop and eat. Giving in to these pressures is a recipe for disaster. If you use up your glycogen stores—the brain and body's fuel—without replenishing it, you'll "bonk." Basically, your brain and body will stop working together to get you moving.

Instead of waiting until you're hungry to eat, pay attention to the time and eat every hour or so. This doesn't mean you have to sit down and cook a pot of spaghetti—just get something in your system. Alternatively, stop to snack at designated spots such as trail junctions, overlooks, lakes, or other obvious or scenic areas. If you're tracking your distance with a GPS, you can keep an eye on the mileage and pause every 2 or 3 miles to snack.

Foods heavy in carbohydrates will fuel you for your hike, but they can feel heavy in your stomach when you're on the move. Don't eliminate them from your pack—just eat small portions often so your body has a chance to digest them. They are still the best choice for keeping your energy up.

Premade and processed foods are convenient, but try to include some unprocessed, natural foods in your pack, as well. They are a lot more appetizing, so you're more apt to stop and eat them. Think about it: Would you be more likely to stop for a trail bar with a bottle of water or a peanut butter and jelly sandwich with chocolate milk?

Recommended foods for the trail include the following:

Protein bars: These are convenient snacks for when you're on the go. Check the ingredients and opt for bars that are low in sugar and high in nutrition, with whole grains, dark chocolate, fruit, nuts, and seeds. Don't confuse them with energy bars, which can be loaded with sugar. Energy bars give you a quick burst of energy, but just like energy drinks, the effect is short-lived and will not sustain you.

Sandwiches and wraps: A sandwich may not be as convenient as a bar, but it's a delicious switch from dried or processed foods. Make them with whole-grain bread, bagels, English muffins, rolls, or tortillas, and pack in lots of fresh vegetables plus spicy, salty, or sweet dressings (but not too much or it will make the bread soggy). Alternatively, pack the veggies and dressing separately from the sandwich and add them when you're ready to eat. If you're going on a long hike in hot weather, add a small cold pack to keep the sandwich fresh.

Fruits, nuts, and seeds: Fresh or dried bananas, apples, and berries mixed with nuts and seeds make a tasty trail mix. Peanut butter crackers combine carbs, fats, and protein for a salty snack that's nutritious, delicious, and satisfying. If you eat a lot of dried fruits such as raisins or dates, drink more water so your body can rehydrate them without dehydrating you.

Carry a variety of sweet and salty foods with strong flavors. Bland foods won't whet your appetite, and you need to be motivated to stop and eat. Sweets like gummies and energy blocks are okay, but only when used in moderation. Don't depend on them for long-lasting energy or nutrition, and don't include them as part of your daily nutritional or caloric requirements. They are basically empty calories. Always have a few extra

Bars and blocks are convenient when you're on the go, but include whole foods like fruits, veggies, and sandwiches in your pack, too.

protein bars in your pack in addition to your regular meals and snacks. That way, if the hike is longer or more difficult than you expect, you'll have enough food to keep you going.

Eat After the Hike

When you pack for a hike, remember to also include food for *after* your hike. Whether it's a snack at the trailhead or in the car, a cooked meal at camp, or a restaurant meal on the way home, your body needs to be refueled as soon as possible—preferably within an hour after your hike. Recovery drinks and snacks are the most convenient post-hike options and can be especially dense in the nutrients your body needs. They do tend to be more expensive and not as appetizing as their "real food" counterparts. Not surprisingly, the same foods that keep you healthy before and during a hike also help you recover. Look for foods high in protein and complex carbohydrates and stay away from high-fat, sugary options.

If you stop at a restaurant on the way home, build a meal of protein, carbs, and a little fat. A clean protein like beans, tofu, or plant-based meats paired with a carbohydrate like potatoes, rice, or pasta and a green salad makes a great post-hike meal. For dessert, choose fruit or dark chocolate.

If you don't have time for a full meal after your hike, at least have a good-size snack handy to eat in the car. Chocolate soy, oat, or almond milk coupled with whole-grain chips can tide you over for a short time until you have time to sit down and eat.

Eating on Multiday Trips

On backpacking trips where time is at a premium and you want to go fast and light, you can rely on prepackaged, freeze-dried food for breakfast and dinner. Complete meals are available at most outdoor retailers and even at big-box stores. Vegan and vegetarian options are sold at some stores and are more readily available online. In addition to these full meals, look for instant soups and pasta and bean mixes.

While these meals can be quick and convenient, they're also expensive, and some come with a lot of excess packaging, which you have to pack out. Some have a lot of preservatives, and if you're eating them night after night, you'll lose your taste for them. A less expensive and often more nutritious option is to bring your own ingredients and make your own recipes. Instant potatoes, quick-cooking noodles, precooked packaged rice, breads, bouillon, fresh or packaged vegetables, packaged proteins, herbs, and spices can be combined to create delicious hot meals. Add a mix of sweet and salty foods that don't require preparation like fruits, nuts, seeds, dark chocolate, and jerky. Make sure you have enough food to cover meals and snacks for the whole trip, plus a little extra in case your trip takes longer than expected.

Eating at Camp

If you are car-camping or doing a multiday hike with a leisurely schedule, where carrying some extra weight isn't an issue, your food-choice options are practically unlimited. Still, make sure they're nutritious picks. Again, combine complex carbohydrates, proteins, and fats, plus some sodium to keep your electrolytes in balance. Following are a few ideas to consider:

Breakfast: Many people enjoy a hot cup of tea or coffee to start the day. Use tea bags and instant coffee, or bring a French press or coffee-maker made especially for camping. The hot water wakes up your digestive system and will help you get the morning bowel movement out of the way so you can enjoy your hike without having to stop and dig a hole. Remember to pack the ground coffee, sugar or other sweetener, and powdered creamer if that's your preference. Instant oatmeal, cream of wheat, quinoa, grits, and granola topped with dried or fresh fruit are quick and easy to prepare. A protein bar or slice of whole-grain bread topped with nut butter adds protein and fats. If you have the time, the cooler, and the cookware, you can go all out with a full breakfast of pancakes, French toast, bacon or sausage, eggs, hash browns, and toast with jam. Vegan eggs, butter, and breakfast meats hold up well in a cooler. Breakfast burritos are another option. If you want to get an early start on your hike, skip the big breakfast and go for fast and easy—coffee, instant oatmeal, fruit, and a bar.

Dinner: Start with a complex carb–rich base of pasta, rice, or potatoes. Traditional pasta can take a while to cook, but you can shorten it by opting for dried Asian-style noodles like ramen, rice vermicelli, and buckwheat soba. Precooked, packaged rice combinations that include brown rice, quinoa, garlic, spices, and even beans take just minutes to heat with a little water. For mashed potatoes, go with potato flakes that cook fast in boiling water. Add packaged or canned vegetables and proteins (don't forget the can opener), plus some instant gravy or bouillon for more flavor. Serve in a bowl or wrapped in a tortilla.

HOW MANY CALORIES DO I NEED?

Your metabolism—how fast you process food for energy—has a lot to say about how many calories you need to maintain your current weight. So does your typical level of activity and the intensity and distance of your hike. To estimate your caloric requirements and how they're affected by hiking, just figure out your basal metabolic rate (BMR), your average weekly level of activity, and the metabolic equivalent of task (MET) of your hike.

Basal Metabolic Rate

Your BMR is how many calories you burn with absolutely no activity. The formula for women is different than for men because we tend to have a higher body fat to muscle ratio and lower metabolism. The Mifflin-St Jeor formula for calculating your BMR is as follows:

655.1 + (4.35 x weight in pounds) + (4.7 x height in inches) – (4.7 x age)

Once you know your BMR, you can use that number to figure out your daily caloric requirement.

Daily Caloric Requirement

Your BMR multiplied times a number associated with your weekly activity level gives you an estimate of how many calories you need to consume *daily* to maintain your current weight. Here are the multipliers:

> Not active = 1.2
> Light exercise 1 to 3 days a week = 1.37
> Moderate exercise 3 to 5 days a week = 1.55
> Hard exercise 5 to 7 days a week = 1.725
> Extremely active with hard exercise 7 days a week = 1.9

How Hiking Affects Your Caloric Requirements

If you increase your level of activity, you have to increase your calorie intake in order to prevent weight loss. Figuring out how many calories you burn on a hike is tough to estimate. Depending on your BMR, how fast you move, the difficulty of your hike, and the weight of your pack, you could burn just 100 calories an hour or more than 1,000. You can get a rough idea if you know the intensity of your hike, and your heart rate is a good indicator. To figure out how that works into the calculation, start out with your maximum heart rate, or 220 minus your age. Hiking at *moderate* intensity gets your heart rate to between 64 percent and 76 percent of your maximum beats per minute (max bpm). Hiking at *high* intensity gets your heart rate to between 77 percent and 93 percent of your max bpm. You can track your heart rate with a heart monitor, smartphone app, or smartwatch. If you don't want to track it, just pay attention to how you feel—your pounding heart, respiration (how hard and fast you're breathing), sweating, and muscle fatigue.

Knowing how intense your hike is, you can assign a *metabolic equivalent of task*, or MET, which is related to the amount of oxygen used to perform a task. Without getting too technical, we can assume that a moderate-intensity hike has a MET of 3 to 6 and a high-intensity hike has a MET of 6 to 9. Again, these are rough numbers. But if you want to figure out how many calories you burn on a hike, plug your BMR and METs into the following formula:

BMR x METs ÷ 24 x duration of activity in hours = Calories

Do you have to do the math before you go for a hike? Of course not. But this should give you an idea of how your activity level affects the number of calories you need, information that will come in handy as you plan your meals. Pay attention to what you eat, how much you eat, and how you feel during and after a hike. Over time, you'll figure out how much you need to maintain your weight and your energy, and to fully recover.

TAKE STEPS

1. Make a grocery list of foods to pick up for before, during, and after your next hike. Check the aisles of your grocery store for foods like peanut butter crackers and other tasty snacks.

2. Try a variety of protein bars for snacking and dehydrated meals for camping. Don't buy too many of one particular brand of bars or meals—you may not like them. Test different brands to find which ones taste best and make you feel good.

3. For variety, think of some foods you can make from ingredients instead of relying on instant.

Otina Fox takes a break on a ski tour to step off the trail and use her feminine urinary director, or FUD.

PHOTO COURTESY OF OTINA FOX

CHAPTER 8

PERSONAL CARE

KEEPING YOURSELF CLEAN in the wild is a balance between what you already do in your bathroom at home and what's practical on the trail. This chapter covers what you need to know about being clean and feeling good without sacrificing health and safety. The first order of business is where and how to *do* your business: bathroom basics.

BATHROOM BASICS

Not all trailheads and fewer trails have restrooms. Before you go on a hike, check the trailhead description to see if there's a pit toilet. Use the toilet at home, and if you have a long drive, stop at a gas station or grocery store. Pack a toilet kit for the trail. After a few trips, you'll be a backcountry bathroom pro.

Your Toilet Kit

You can buy a premade toilet kit, but putting together your own "bathroom in a bag" is cheaper and lets you pick the products you really like. Your kit can be as simple as a zippered bag containing toilet paper, premoistened wipes, hand sanitizer, and whatever you use for periods. Go with unscented products to avoid attracting insects or animals. Used toilet paper, wipes, pads, and tampons need to be packed out. Carry a second, disposable bag for them. On hot days, double-bag waste to prevent odors from leaking out. Keep your toilet kit in the top part of your pack.

Get a feminine urinary director (FUD), which allows you to pee standing up without dropping your drawers. For chafing between your thighs, under your arms, or around your nipples, add an anti-chafing stick. Before you use any of these products in the backcountry, test them at home to

Buy a toilet kit or build your own, with wipes, a feminine urinary director, a trowel, and more.

make sure you don't have an allergic reaction to the ingredients. Add a small lightweight trowel to dig holes for pooping in, but never bury anything else such as paper waste. If you carry an ice axe, you can leave the trowel at home.

Some areas require you to pack out your poop. If that's the case, carry a premade, disposable waste bag (WAG bag, short for Waste Alleviation and Gelling). You can pick these up at any outdoor gear shop or order them online. Typically, you would use one WAG bag per poop, so carry enough to cover your trip. WAG bags usually come with wipes and are self-contained.

Dispose of the used items—TP, wipes, pads, tampons, WAG bag—as soon as you get home so they don't stink up your pack, and replace depleted items before your next hike.

Pit Toilets

Outdoor toilet enclosures are intentionally dark so as not to attract flies. They do not have sinks, but most have toilet paper, and some are equipped with automatic lights and hand sanitizer units.

Bring your toilet kit with you into the pit toilet in case the dispensers are empty. At night, bring a headlamp. Keep everything attached to you or in a zippered pocket so you don't accidentally drop something in the toilet. The toilet seat should be down, so use a bit of toilet paper to protect your hand and lift the seat. If the toilet's full due to area flooding, you may want to go outside instead. A full toilet can create splash-back.

Don't throw anything in the toilet except for toilet paper: no premoistened wipes, no feminine pads, no tampons, and no trash. These prevent decomposition, and someone may have to physically remove these items. When you're done, put the seat down to allow the toilet to work properly and shut the enclosure door to keep animals out.

Some pit toilets have no enclosures, so you're sitting on a seat or a plank, going into a hole in the ground. The same rules apply here: Make sure everything is attached to you, and don't drop anything into the pit.

Peeing and Pooping on the Trail

Using the trailhead toilet will limit trailside potty stops, but if you're out for more than a couple of hours, plan to go freestyle. You can either drop your pack on the side of the trail or bring it with you, but grab your toilet kit before heading off to your potty spot. Don't ever go to the bathroom right on the trail.

If you're hiking near a stream or lake, hike off-trail in the opposite direction and try to put at least 200 feet between yourself and the water to avoid sullying the groundwater and contaminating lakes and rivers that are home to wildlife and may be your source of drinking and cooking water. If possible, find a spot at least 50 feet from the trail. In the forest, you can usually find privacy behind trees, bushes, or boulders. Above tree line, you may not have any privacy at all. When space or privacy are limited, take turns going while another person plays lookout on the trail to warn you about approaching hikers who could surprise you midstream.

Pee on dirt or on rocks, but don't squat too low or pee too hard or you'll get splashed. Avoid peeing on plants, tundra, and cryptobiotic or biological crust soil, which could destroy these natural environments or attract animals that could destroy them. Avoid peeing on your boots, socks, and pants. This is where a FUD really comes in handy. You simply unzip your pants or pull them down in the front, press the large end of the funnel against your body, and go. FUDs work well for rock climbing and rope team glacier travel, too, because you can use them without getting out of your harness or separating from your team. Before using your FUD in the backcountry, practice with it at home—first in the shower, and then in the toilet—to get used to peeing while standing up and perfecting your aim.

Animals such as goats and marmots are attracted to the salt in sweat and urine. In high-use areas, they may be accustomed to hikers and can be aggressive about staking a claim on your pee. Be aware of your environment. If you feel threatened, wait until you're in a safer place.

If you have to poop, dig a hole in the dirt about 6 inches deep. Do your business, wipe, stash your used paper or wipes away in your toilet kit, and cover the hole with dirt. Some people refuse to pack out their soiled toilet paper, thinking it will decompose in the wild. In fact, it can take years for paper to break down. In the meantime, animals could dig it up. It could blow around and get caught in tree branches. Used TP could even end up in a nearby stream—your water source. Leaving paper and any other toilet products behind is a rookie move in the backcountry. Be a woman and pack it out.

Peeing and Pooping at Camp

Even if you don't usually get up in the middle of the night to go pee at home, you'll probably have to go when you camp. Altitude, cold, exercise, and all that water you drank during the day combine to make nighttime potty breaks inevitable. Limit them by going before you crawl into your sleeping bag.

Have your headlamp, jacket, sandals or booties, and toilet kit handy for nighttime potty breaks. Find your way to the nearest pit toilet. If there's no toilet, locate a spot at least 50 feet from the tent before you go to bed so you can find it easily in the dark.

Sometimes leaving the tent isn't convenient, like when you're surrounded by other campers and there's no privacy, or when the weather is so bad that you don't want to go out. You can learn to pee with a FUD while kneeling or lying down, but you'll want to practice this at home first, in the bathtub. Using a FUD in the tent also requires a pee bottle clearly marked with a big X of duct tape so you don't mistake it for drinking water in the dark. Use an old water bottle and make sure it's big enough to hold your typical output. Remember to empty your pee bottle in the morning far from camp.

Managing Your Period

Use the same menstrual products on the trail that you use at home. The only caveat is to avoid scented products that can attract animals and insects. Tampons stay put better than pads, and some women prefer them for long hikes and multiday trips. Depending on your flow, you may be able to get by with just one tampon for a day hike. If you're worried about leaks, add a thin pad as a backup. Tampons take up little space in your pack and some are made with no applicator, so there's less weight and less to pack out, too. You will probably get your hands dirty when changing a tampon, so make sure to carry wipes in your toilet kit. Some people prefer pads over tampons because they're easier to change. Whether you go with tampons or pads, bring enough for the days and nights that you will be away.

A popular option is the menstrual cup. Depending on the manufacturer and your flow, you might be able to go for twelve hours before emptying a cup, making it convenient for long days on the trail. Dump your cup like you would solid waste, in a cathole, and rinse it thoroughly before reinserting. Follow the manufacturer's guidelines for changing your tampon and disinfecting your cup to avoid toxic shock syndrome (TSS). If you get cramps, headaches, or other symptoms around your period, add whatever pain reliever or other meds you typically use to your first-aid kit. All disposable feminine products have to be packed out, so bring a ziplock bag that's large enough to hold used TP, wipes, and tampons or pads. Between menstruation cycles, wearing a light-flow feminine pad to catch urine leaks and stray drippage after bathroom breaks eliminates the need to wipe with toilet paper every time you pee.

Toilet Kit Checklist
- ☐ Zippered or resealable bag or pouch
- ☐ Disposable double-bag for used items
- ☐ Toilet paper
- ☐ Premoistened unscented wipes
- ☐ Hand sanitizer
- ☐ Menstrual cup, pads, or tampons
- ☐ Feminine urinary director (FUD): Pack this outside your toilet kit in a hip-belt pouch or side pocket of your pack so you can get to it without having to take off your pack.
- ☐ Unscented anti-chafing stick, cream, or gel
- ☐ Small trowel
- ☐ WAG bag(s)

WILD, CLEAN, AND FEELING GOOD!

However you feel about your appearance, taking care of your hair, skin, nails, and teeth in the backcountry makes you feel better and keeps you safer, too. Bad hygiene can lead to infections, and bacteria transmitted from hands to eyes and mouth can cause problems like diarrhea. You will get dirty—that's a given. Dust, dirt, twigs, bugs, sweat, and snot end up on your skin, in your hair, and between your toes. If you're bushwhacking off-trail, there may be blood. Unless you are car-camping near hot showers or packing in a solar shower, you'll depend on a cleanup kit to stay clean. And if you do want to keep up appearances, you can do that, too.

Your Cleanup Kit

Just like a toilet kit, you can build your own cleanup kit from your favorite products. Start with a zippered or resealable bag and add an extra bag (or double bag) to dispose of all the used items like tissues, premoist-ened wipes, cotton swabs, toothpicks, and dental floss. What you put in your kit is up to you and your personal preferences. If you're hiking to high altitude, don't use products that come in pressurized containers in your toilet and cleanup kits, as they can burst in your pack. Just like your toilet kit, dispose of the used items as soon as you get home and replace depleted items before your next hike.

HAIR

There are no magic tricks to make your hair shower-clean or blown-out thick and shiny on the trail, but you can maintain it for days with just a few items. Tame long hair with a headband or bandana, or just tie it back in a braid or ponytail to keep it off your face. A buff can be twisted into a cap or band too. You can also wear a visor and tuck your hair up under it, or in the winter, use a headband-style ear warmer. If you have bangs, make sure they're not so long that they get in your eyes. If they are, trim them or wear a hair band to keep them off your face. Loop an extra hair tie on your pack's haul loop so you always have it handy to tie your hair back.

If you're camping out, comb out your hair at night to get the tangles out. A wide-toothed comb or small detangling brush is best to prevent breakage. If your hair is particularly oily, you can use a dry shampoo at night or in the morning. Whatever you decide, keep it simple. You shouldn't be spending all your backcountry time stressing over your tresses.

SKIN

Just like hair, keep your skin routine simple. Start with sunscreen on your face and any exposed areas and apply it regularly. Bonus points if your sunscreen doubles as a moisturizer. Apply lip balm that contains sunscreen, too, to protect against sunburned or chapped lips, and keep it handy for reapplying after you eat.

Perfumes, colognes, and other unnatural fragrances in the backcountry can attract insects and animals and may be offensive to other hikers. If you're worried about how you smell, use some unscented deodorant. Better yet, get used to your natural odor and the odors of other people. Most healthy people do not smell that bad, even after a few days.

What you put on your face beyond sunscreen is up to you, but keep the products to a minimum. If you're used to full-face makeup—foundation, blush, lipstick, and more—prepare to be liberated from that time-consuming and totally-unnecessary-in-the-wild routine. Spending time outside makes you look good, and the more time you spend out there, the more good-looking you will become. At least, that's been my experience. Instead of cosmetics, boost your natural beauty from within with exercise, nutrition, hydration, fresh air, and fun to put color in your cheeks, a sparkle in your eyes, and a healthy glow all over your face.

Many women skip makeup completely in the backcountry, but if you want to wear it, go easy. In the bright light of the big outdoors, a little goes a long way. A dash of concealer, smudge of blush, and swipe of mascara are enough to ease you from your usual daily makeup to a fresh-faced look that will feel better and be easier to maintain on the trail. Choose products that are unscented, hold up in the heat, and don't clog your pores. Stay away from sticks and powders that melt or leak into your pack. If you wear mascara, a tubing type is less likely to smear and comes off with a wet wipe. If you're camping, gently remove the makeup, sweat, and dirt from your face at night with moisturizing wipes. Pat on a light moisturizer and get your beauty sleep.

NAILS

Long fingernails collect dirt and germs, catch on pack pulls, and break on rocks and branches. Long toenails are also a problem on the trail, especially on a steep downhill hike where they hit the front of your boots with every step. Keep your nails clipped and carry nail clippers and a file or emery board to take care of hangnails and rough spots. If you wear nail polish, go with something durable that won't flake off the first day. Don't expect to be touching up polish at camp or on the trail. Clip your toenails and fingernails two days before your hike and right after you shower while they're soft and touch up rough edges with an emery board the next day to prevent snags.

TEETH

For camping trips, bring a toothbrush and unscented toothpaste. Step away from camp with your brush, paste, and a bottle of water for rinsing. Avoid spitting onto plants and aim for rocks and dirt. On the trail, a flosser, which is a small pick strung with a bit of floss, is all you need to dislodge chunks of food between brushings.

Other Personal Items

If you wear contact lenses, carry a lens case and eye drops, and bring a small bottle of saline on camping trips. Lens cases tend to leak, so bag them up. For eyeglasses, bring something to wipe them clean. For camping, have a case to keep them safe. Consider carrying an eyeglass repair kit, or just bring some fishing line, scissors, and duct tape for emergency repairs.

Keep your birth control in your cleanup kit. If you store these items in your first-aid kit you may forget about them, and if you put them in your toilet kit, they could get damp or stinky. You'll be digging into your cleanup kit at least once a day, decreasing the odds of forgetting to take a pill. Alternatively, you can opt for long-term birth control such as an IUD, vaginal ring, patch, implant, or injection, but should you engage in sex at camp, you will still need additional protection like a condom to guard against STDs.

Clean-Up Kit Checklist

- ☐ Hair ties, scarf, buff, or headband
- ☐ Wide-toothed comb or detangling brush
- ☐ Dry shampoo
- ☐ Tissues
- ☐ Premoistened unscented wipes
- ☐ Hand sanitizer
- ☐ Facial sunscreen that doesn't sting your eyes
- ☐ Lip balm with sunscreen
- ☐ Soap that doesn't require rinsing, or at least thorough rinsing
- ☐ Moisturizer (unscented)
- ☐ Deodorant (unscented)
- ☐ Cotton swabs
- ☐ Makeup (unscented)
- ☐ Small mirror, such as the top half of a powder compact, for applying facial products

- ☐ Nail clippers, file, emery board
- ☐ Toothpicks, dental floss, or flossers
- ☐ Toothbrush
- ☐ Toothpaste (unscented)
- ☐ Lens case and saline solution, if you wear contact lenses
- ☐ Eyeglass case, cloth, and repair kit if you wear glasses
- ☐ Birth control / STD protection

HIKING, CAMPING, AND SEX

Intimacy in the backcountry isn't common simply because people are tired, sweaty, hungry, thirsty, and focused on other matters. If you choose to engage in frisky behavior, be respectful of other people and their sensitivity to public shows of affection. Keep it in the tent and keep it quiet. By the way, agreeing to share a tent with a guy—or another woman—is not an invitation to sex. People of all genders share tents with no expectations at all from the other party; they are simply sharing a tent for sleeping. People used to backcountry travel understand this, but if you wind up sharing a tent with someone who doesn't, clue them in immediately. Inappropriate or unwanted affection isn't cool anywhere.

TAKE STEPS

1. Build a toilet kit and a cleanup kit and figure out where to put them in your pack.
2. Buy a FUD and practice using it in the shower or toilet at home.
3. Think about what you're currently using for periods and birth control and consider whether you might try something more convenient for multiday trips.

Lisa Heckel—here, on the summit of Unnamed 13,500 and en route to Twining Peak, Independence Pass, Colorado—balances her backcountry passion with bicycling and yoga to maintain a healthy mind, body, and soul.
PHOTO BY DARIN BAKER

CHAPTER 9

STAYING HEALTHY

PREVENTIVE CARE keeps common illnesses and injuries at bay. We'll talk about problems that require first aid in chapter 10. For now, learn the symptoms of mild health issues, how to prevent them, and how to treat them before they require emergency care.

HEADACHES

Headaches can be a symptom of dehydration or low blood sugar (hypoglycemia). Eat and drink at regular intervals, even when you're not hungry

LISA HECKEL started hiking, camping, and mountaineering after graduating from college. Since then, she's summited all the Colorado 14ers and the state's highest 100 peaks, the "Centennials," and she's currently working toward completing the 500-plus-mile Colorado Trail from Denver to Durango. Over the years, Lisa's volunteered as a basic mountaineering and backpacking instructor for the Colorado Mountain Club. Between hikes and climbs, she cross-trains on her bicycle and gives thanks to her body through yoga practice. She's also a faculty member of the physical therapist assistant program at Pueblo Community College, where she helps students achieve their passion for truly making a difference in someone's life. Lisa fosters cats for Safe Place for Pets, an organization that supports terminally ill people and their families in rehoming their pets. One of her favorite quotes is by John Muir: "And into the forest I go to lose my mind and find my soul."

or thirsty. Headaches can also indicate high-altitude sickness or acute mountain sickness (AMS), discussed in chapter 21, "High-Altitude Mountaineering." Drinking and eating can sometimes ward off the symptoms, but if they persist, head down to a lower altitude. Some women suffer from exercise-induced headaches. Take an over-the-counter pain reliever for temporary relief, and for serious headaches or migraines, see your doctor.

MUSCLE ACHES AND SORENESS

Any time you push your body to do more than it's used to, it responds in good ways and bad. Hiking will make you stronger and improve your cardio health, but you may suffer a little along the way. Lessen the inevitable soreness by getting into shape with regular exercise on your "off days," including strength training, stretching, and cardiovascular workouts. Before a big hike, do some stretching, focusing on the muscles that take the brunt of the work: back, shoulders, and legs, including hip flexors, quadriceps, hamstrings, and calves. Gently stretch after your hike, too. Never "bounce" into stretches or overextend your limbs, which can cause muscle tears and joint injuries. Get plenty of rest before and after hikes to allow your body to recover, and use an over-the-counter pain reliever as needed. For more on physical preparedness, see chapter 16, "Training."

MUSCLE CRAMPS

Cramps are a sustained muscle contraction often caused by dehydration, an electrolyte imbalance, or muscle fatigue. Eat, drink, exercise regularly, and stretch before and after hikes to ward off cramping. If you get a cramp during a hike or at night in the tent, massage the area to relax the muscle and get some food and water or a sports drink into your system.

EXHAUSTION

Wearing yourself out on the trail can be caused by not eating or drinking enough, pushing yourself too hard or for too long without a break, and by going into a hike without enough rest. Again, eat and drink often and take breaks on the trail. If you're still hiking to your destination and you're wiped out, stop and rest, then consider turning back. You won't suddenly be reenergized at the halfway point (the destination), and you still have to get back to the trail-head. Avoid exhaustion by getting plenty of sleep before and after every hike. If you're camping out and you're a light sleeper, pitch your tent in a quiet spot away from other campers, or wear earplugs. If there's a stream along the route, make your campsite nearby (but not too close). The rushing water acts as white noise to drown out nighttime noises. Over-the-counter sleep aids are another option, but read the directions so you know how long the effects last. You don't

Taking a break is the smart way to avoid exhaustion. Beth Balser, Jan Ruberg, and Linda Parobek relax at camp after a long day on Blue Lakes Trail in Colorado's Rawah Wilderness.
PHOTO BY LEIGH PETERSON

want to start a hike feeling groggy in the morning. Avoid sleep aids completely if you're sleeping at altitude (more on this in chapter 21). Finally, avoid caffeine and alcohol. Both can interfere with your sleep, leading to exhaustion on the trail.

GAS

Gas expressed as burps and farts is common during any exercise, more so when you move in a way that twists or compresses your core. When you breathe hard or gulp water, air gets into your gastrointestinal tract. You can decrease gas buildup by breathing in through your nose and out of your mouth, but you probably won't eliminate it completely. If you're really bothered by excessive gas, look at your diet. Certain foods such as high-fiber vegetables have a gassy effect on some people. Gas expulsion often increases when you hike uphill, and at altitude. This is because the motion of your body as you ascend compresses your stomach and intestines, squeezing the air out. At altitude, Boyle's Law also comes into play, where the higher you go, the more the gas in your body expands. High-altitude flatus expulsion (HAFE) doesn't always end after the air pressure inside and outside your body "equalizes." It can persist for hours after a high-altitude hike, possibly due to gas buildup in your bloodstream being released into your GI tract. No one really knows for sure, and there's not much you can do about it except learn to live with it.

CONSTIPATION AND DIARRHEA

Tummy troubles on the trail can usually be avoided with a little preparation. Before your hike, avoid trying new foods or any foods that have caused you problems in the past. Stick as closely as possible to your regular diet so your body isn't shocked into dealing with something different. Hydrate and include plenty of fiber in your pre-hike meals.

If you're constipated while camping, get up early and have a hot beverage to wake up your system and get you going. If the condition persists, you can try a natural remedy like prunes, raisins, or herbal tea containing senna. Senna tea contains anthraquinones, powerful laxatives derived from the senna plant. If you get constipated a lot on your camping trips, pack a laxative in your first-aid kit. Test any laxative at home before using it on the trail to see how your body reacts. If you take something for constipation, give it time to work—at least a day. Don't be tempted to double up on doses or you could end up with diarrhea.

Try to empty your bowels before you hit the trail. If you have diarrhea, take an over-the-counter remedy to get you through the day. Diarrhea can be caused by exercise, but it could also be a symptom of a more serious issue like giardiasis, cryptosporidiosis, or other illnesses caused by bacteria, viruses, and parasites. Always treat or boil your water for drinking and cooking and practice safe backcountry bathroom habits. Untreated, diarrhea can lead to dehydration. If you're prone to "the runs," pack an antidiarrheal in your first-aid kit and extra bathroom supplies to clean yourself up, and drink throughout the day to stay hydrated.

BLISTERS AND CALLUSES

Blisters on your feet are usually caused by shoes or boots that don't fit right. They can also appear if you haven't taken time to break in new footwear before wearing it on a long hike. Prevent blisters with good hiking shoes and socks that fit, with no hot spots. Wear new hiking shoes for several short trips—even around the block or local park—before committing them to a long trek. Carry moleskin in your first-aid kit and use it to prevent blisters, and to protect them from more abrasion if they do occur. Be sure to read the instructions first, and never place the adhesive surface directly on the blister, which could create additional injury. Instead, cut a hole in the moleskin the size of the blister and place it over the affected area to prevent the inside of the shoe from coming in contact with the blister.

Calluses—the rough layers of skin that develop on your soles—are inevitable if you hike a lot. Unless you're diabetic or have nerve or circulation issues, leave your calluses alone. They provide a layer of protection for your feet, for future hikes. You can get blisters and calluses anywhere your pack or poles rub against your skin. Buy a pack that doesn't rub against your arms or chest and adjust the straps for a good fit. If your trekking poles are causing hand blisters or calluses, try varying your grip, wear gloves, or use moleskin or Band-Aids to protect the sore spots.

SCRATCHES, SCRAPES, CUTS, AND BRUISES

You may head through dense growth at some point on your hike, and you'll get a few scratches. If the terrain is particularly bad, protect yourself with long pants and a long-sleeved shirt or jacket. Superficial scrapes and cuts come with the territory. Wipe off any dirt with a premoistened wipe, treat with an antibacterial cream, and if the cut is open or bleeding, cover it with a Band-Aid. If it's more serious, apply first aid (discussed in chapter 10). Bruising is also common, but you probably won't even notice it until you get home from your hike. Treatment is rarely necessary. Unless you have a serious contusion or head injury, allow bruises to heal on their own.

BUG BITES

Bugs are more common in certain parts of the country, like the South and the East Coast, but they can appear anywhere, especially in high humidity or near standing water. If you're hiking through a buggy area, wear long pants and a long-sleeved shirt or jacket and use bug spray. In areas where mosquitoes are fierce, consider wearing a *head net*—a hat with netting that goes over your face and neck. Protect your hands with glove liners. After a hike, check your body for ticks, and if you find one, carefully remove with fine-tipped tweezers. Wash the area and the tweezers with soap and water or rubbing alcohol, shower completely when you get home, and do another tick check. See chapter 10 for more on tick bites.

SUNBURN

Apply 30 SPF (or higher) sunscreen early, liberally, and often. Look for sports solutions that are less likely to sweat off, and if you can't reach some places, like your upper back, use a spray or get a friend to help. Apply to all exposed skin: face, neck, ears, arms, back, shoulders, and legs. Reapply according to the directions, and more often if you're

sweating it off. When you sweat, the sunscreen on your forehead can slide into your eyes; if it stings, get a second, sting-free sunscreen made especially for faces.

When you're outside for hours, you can get sunburned in unexpected places. If you part your hair, the skin exposed at the part can get burned, so either apply sunscreen

Sunscreen and anti-chafing products prevent skin irritation on the trail.

or wear a hat. Hiking on snow, the sun doesn't just shine down on you; it's also reflected off the snow, and can burn the inside of your nose and roof of your mouth. If you're going to be on snow all day, apply sunscreen in your nostrils. Use your thumb so you don't go too far; you don't need sunscreen in your entire nasal cavity, just the lower part. To protect the roof of your mouth, breathe in through your nose and out through your mouth to limit how long your mouth is open, or just wear a buff over your mouth.

Don't neglect your eyes. Solar radiation can cause permanent eye damage and the effects are enhanced on snow, with the sun's rays beating down from above and reflecting up into your face. Wear sunglasses.

COLD AND HEAT

Changes in air temperature and in body temperature make clothing adjustments necessary on the trail. On cool or cold days, avoid getting wet, which can bring your temperature down fast. If you get cold, stop and add a layer. Your body needs fuel to regulate its temperature, so don't skip snacks and meals. Instead, put on a warm jacket, eat, sip a hot beverage, and get moving again. If you're getting too warm, remove layers, snack, and drink something cool. For a quick cooldown, moisten your hat or buff with some water. If you have a cold pack in your food, put it against your neck for relief. Raising and lowering zippers can help you adjust while you're on the move. Excessive heat can lead to heatstroke or hyperthermia, and excessive cold can lead to hypothermia (discussed in chapter 10).

WINDBURN

High, sustained winds, especially in cold weather, can injure your skin. Cover all exposed skin, including your head. A buff, snug hat or cap, sunglasses or goggles, and, if necessary, a facemask, should cover your face completely in high winds, but check for gaps and seal them off with more clothing. Extreme cold and wind can cause frostnip and frostbite, discussed in the next chapter.

Jean Aschenbrenner heads for Missouri Mountain wearing prescription mountaineering sunglasses and a homemade nose guard to protect her eyes and skin from the brilliant Colorado sunshine. PHOTO BY KEN NOLAN

TAKE STEPS

1. On your next hike, pay attention to how you feel. Be proactive about self-care during and after the trip.
2. Pay attention to your hiking partners, too. You might notice that they're getting sunburned or dehydrated before they do. After you've done a lot of trips with a partner, you will be able to tell when they're acting out of character, which could signal a problem that needs attention.
3. If you're a little sore, bruised, or scraped up from your last trip, congratulations. You're pushing yourself a little harder, getting stronger, and giving your immune system a workout, too. Feel free to pat yourself on the back (if you're not too sore).

Emergency services aren't close or convenient in the backcountry. Here, the author is on Ellingwood Point's southwest ridge, Colorado.
PHOTO BY DOUG HATFIELD

CHAPTER 10

FIRST AID

WHILE TAKING EVERY precaution lowers your risk of getting sick or hurt, there is no guarantee that you won't suffer illness or injury on the trail. In the backcountry, you don't have immediate access to medical personnel. If you're able to get a call out on your cell, Search and Rescue or emergency medical services (EMS) may not reach you for hours, or even days. You don't have to be a paramedic to enjoy the wild, but at a minimum, be prepared to administer first aid. This chapter is an introduction to the subject and does not cover serious injuries. Reading it does not certify you as a first-aid specialist. If you plan to spend a lot of time in the backcountry, stay up-to-date with regular first-aid education and get some hands-on training.

FIRST-AID KIT

Buy a premade first-aid kit or build your own, adding items depending on your needs and first-aid skills. Put everything in a water-repellent bag and review your kit every season to replace expired meds and depleted items. Here are some items to consider for your kit:

First-Aid Kit Basics

> Your personal medications, especially prescription meds and instructions for their use. That way, if you're unconscious and someone has to take care of you, they will be better equipped to assess and treat you. If your medical needs include EpiPens,

inhalers, or other items that you need immediate access to, consider carrying them outside your kit, where you can get to them faster. You may want to let someone in your party know where they are and what they're for in case you lose consciousness.

> A pain reliever/NSAID (nonsteroidal anti-inflammatory drug) such as ibuprofen, naproxen, or aspirin to reduce inflammation, swelling, and fever, and relieve minor aches and pains. Note that acetaminophen is not an NSAID and does not treat inflammation.
> Antiseptic wipes for cleaning cuts
> Rubbing alcohol for cleaning tick bites
> Moleskin for treating blisters and hot spots
> Hand sanitizer to clean your hands before treating a wound
> Topical triple antibiotic ointment such as Neosporin to prevent infection in cuts, scrapes, and small wounds and as an antifungal treatment
> Adhesive waterproof bandages for cuts and scrapes
> Sterile gauze pads for large cuts, scrapes, and wounds
> Skin closures or butterfly bandages for treating open cuts
> Surgical, silicone, or athletic tape for securing bandages
> Tweezers for removing ticks, splinters, and cactus spines
> Hydrocortisone cream to treat itching from insect bites or rashes from contact with poison ivy and other irritants
> Antihistamine such as Benadryl to treat allergies and reduce itching and other effects of certain bug bites
> Antidiarrheal tablets for diarrhea
> Laxative tablets for constipation
> A card or small notebook with your personal information, such as your name, age, height, weight, gender, allergies, prescription meds, and emergency contact information. If you have to be rescued, this will help Search and Rescue and EMS personnel prepare for your evacuation and treatment.
> The notebook along with a pen or pencil can also be used to write down information about someone who needs to be evacuated. If you have to go for help, jot down the injured person's approximate height, weight, location, and details of their injuries and carry it instead of trusting all that information to memory.

> If you're allergic to anything, include a note on that as well. For example, if you're allergic to iodine—a common treatment for water in the backcountry—make sure that this is noted in your first-aid kit so that if you become injured or unconscious, someone coming to your aid doesn't make you even sicker by administering iodine-treated water.

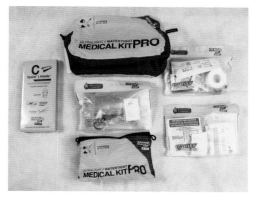

Buy or build a first-aid kit.

Additional First-Aid Kit Items:

> Soap and irrigating water bottle to clean a wound
> Cotton swabs for applying creams
> Hemostatic gauze dressing to control heavy bleeding from a wound
> Kinesiology tape for sore joints and muscles
> Triangular bandage, C-Splint™, and SAM® Splint to immobilize an injured digit or limb. Specialized splints made of soft aluminum, aluminum alloys, and closed-cell foam form a firm support structure for injured bones, joints, and soft tissue.
> Safety pins for fastening cloth bandages and slings
> Scissors for cutting bandages and moleskin
> Nitrile gloves to protect your hands when treating wounds and to keep bacteria on your hands from entering a wound. Nitrile is a thin and flexible, yet durable synthetic rubber that provides protection while allowing full dexterity for treating injuries.
> Oil of cloves for toothache pain relief
> Chemical warmers for quickly warming cold hands and feet

STAY CALM AND ASSESS THE SITUATION

When you have a medical issue in the backcountry, stay calm. The people in your group have varying levels of medical experience, so figure out who's the best person to treat the patient and let them take the lead. Don't add to the conversation unless they ask you to. A sick or hurt person feels vulnerable and may be confused or disoriented. The fewer people they have to interact with, the calmer they'll be.

If no one in your group has any formal medical training, you can take it upon yourself to manage the situation. However, under Good Samaritan laws, you are usually not required to provide first aid. This varies by state and by your relationship to the injured party, so if you don't feel competent or comfortable administering first aid, check your state's law to determine your legal responsibilities.

If you do decide to step up, keep your voice low, steady, confident, and soothing. Talk to the patient but don't get into any scary details about the potential outcome of their sickness or extent of the injury. They are looking to you for help and are susceptible to your words and actions. Your job is to help the person remain calm, treat them, and make the decision to continue, return to the trailhead, or seek professional assistance. What needs to be done depends on the situation, the extent of the injury or illness, and the environment.

Task others in your group with small but helpful jobs. Giving people a sense of purpose will dissuade them from interacting with the patient. Ask them to gather supplies from everyone's first-aid kits, identify your exact GPS coordinates or location on a map, and see if anyone has a satellite messenger, personal locator beacon, or cell service to call 911 in case you need help.

When to Move an Injured Person

If the injury isn't serious, you can move the patient to a place that's stable, level, and out of the elements to treat them. If they have a neck or spine injury, don't move them or you could worsen their injury. However, if they're in imminent danger of additional injury, you *should* move them. For example, if you're under an active rockslide or avalanche, get the patient and yourself out of harm's way before you do anything else.

When to Go for Help

If a person's illness or injury is beyond your ability to properly treat them, get help. If they could incur further injury or their situation could worsen before you can evacuate them to the trailhead, get help. You can request help by cell, satellite messenger, or personal locator beacon. If you have talk or text capability, provide information about your location, including the nearest town and road, the name of the land area, trail, closest trail junction and trailhead, distance from the trailhead, and any landmarks. If you are in a remote area and know the GPS waypoints of your location, that could help Search and Rescue find you a lot faster. Also tell them as much as you can about the patient, including height, weight, gender, age, extent of their illness or injuries, and the time the sickness or injury occurred.

If you have no way to contact emergency assistance, one, or preferably *two*, people—if there are enough in your party—will have to hike far enough back to the trailhead to get cell service or return to the trailhead and drive until they have service or can reach a landline. Whoever goes for help should take all of the information with them, in written form, regarding the location and the victim. If they have gear, clothing, food, and water to spare, borrow these items from them to help care for the sick or injured person. You could both be waiting a long time.

Remind whoever goes for help that they should not risk their own safety on the way. They should also remain calm. Meanwhile, whoever stays with the patient should continue to care for them but not neglect their own needs—eating, drinking, protection from the elements, and rest.

Assess the Person's Illness or Injuries

Sometimes a person's injury or illness is obvious. Other times, a formal assessment is needed to identify the nature and extent of the problem. Ask the person for permission to do this. If they're unconscious or can't speak and are unable to give you permission, bear in mind that in most cases, a state's Good Samaritan law protects you from legal action brought against you by the patient for your assistance. This assumes that you do not provide treatment beyond your level of competence and do not start treatment and then abandon the person. Check your state's laws for specifics.

If they appear unconscious, tap or shake their shoulder and ask them loudly if they are okay. If they don't respond, seek assistance. Then identify what's wrong, prioritize the issues, and treat the person.

CPR and CAB

First, check to see if the person's breathing. They are probably lying on their back, but you can do this in whatever position they're in. Put your ear just above their face and look to see if their chest is rising and falling, listen for the sound of their breath in your ear, and feel for their breath on your cheek.

If they are not breathing *and* you are well-trained and confident in your ability to perform cardiopulmonary resuscitation (CPR), follow your CAB training (compressions, airway, breathing). Currently, the standard is to perform thirty compressions, clear the person's airway, then give two rescue breaths and continue, alternating thirty compressions to two breaths until help arrives. However, standards change over time, so follow whatever is most current.

If they aren't breathing and you are not CPR-trained and confident, lay the person on their back and start chest compressions to get their blood circulating. Kneeling alongside the patient, lean over them so your shoulders are above their chest. Place the heel of one hand on the middle of the person's chest and place your other hand on top of that one, fingers laced. Lock your elbows and press down, then release. Continue to compress the chest and release, pressing down two inches or more at a rate of 100 to 120 compressions per minute. If you need to, use a song to get the rate right—the Bee Gees' "Stayin' Alive," Queen's "Another One Bites the Dust," and Lynyrd Skynyrd's "Sweet Home Alabama" have the right tempo. Ask others in your party to sing so you can save your energy for compressions.

Try to continue compressions until the person shows movement, regains consciousness, or medical assistance arrives. In the backcountry it may be a very long time before help arrives, so there are special considerations for wilderness CPR. No one can continue chest compressions for hours, and you are not required to do so, but try to sustain them for at least thirty minutes. Get others in your party to take over if you get tired. Keep an eye on your environment, too, and discontinue CPR or CAB if doing so puts your own life in danger.

Once the person's heartbeat and breathing are established, treat any other life-threatening symptoms, such as profuse bleeding. Then move on to the other vital signs and do a full body assessment and note your findings. Details for assessing a person injured in a wilderness setting are available in a Wilderness First Aid (WFA) course. If you are not trained, simply note everything you can determine about the person's physical and mental state by observing them and asking them questions. Ask someone in your party to take notes so you can pass them on to Search and Rescue or refer to them for treating the person.

CPR is a basic rescue skill that everyone should learn. Wilderness First Aid isn't necessary, but it could save your life or someone else's and is excellent training for anyone who spends a lot of time in the backcountry.

Following are the most common illnesses and how to treat them. Any of these issues can become much more serious and even result in death. If a person is showing symptoms of a serious sickness or injury, call for help, then begin first aid.

SICKNESS CAUSED BY WATER IMBALANCES

Dehydration

Cause: Not drinking enough water before and during a hike.

Symptoms: Dizziness, confusion, slurred speech, irritability, headache, muscle cramps, rapid breathing, rapid heartbeat, dry heaves or vomiting, not having to pee for long periods of time, dark urine.

Treatment: Drink half a liter of water. Sip another half-liter over about fifteen minutes' time to allow your body time to absorb the water. Follow up with sports drinks or snacks to replace electrolytes. If you're also feeling overheated, get out of the sun and find shade under a tree or beside a cliff. Sit down and rest until you feel well enough to continue.

Overhydration and Hyponatremia

Cause: An imbalance of electrolytes caused by drinking too much water.

Symptoms: Dizziness, confusion, fatigue, nausea, vomiting.

Treatment: Stop drinking water and all other drinks and have a salty snack. Rest until you're feeling well enough to continue.

SICKNESS CAUSED BY HEAT AND COLD

Heat Exhaustion and Hyperthermia

Cause: Overheating caused by the environment or exercise.

Symptoms: Headache, confusion, fatigue, rapid breathing, rapid heartbeat, flushed appearance, vomiting.

Treatment: Get out of the sun, drink fluids, and cool the body externally. Soak a bandana, hat, or buff with water and apply to neck, armpits, back, and groin. Drink cool liquids. If there is no improvement, get medical assistance.

Hypothermia

Cause: Body loses heat faster than it produces it.

Symptoms: Shivering, confusion, skin red and cold to the touch or turning blue.

Treatment: Get out of the elements to a place that's dry and out of the wind. Apply heat packs to neck, armpits, back, and groin. Layer more clothing to help retain heat. Drink warm fluids and eat to warm the body from the inside.

Frostnip and Frostbite

Cause: Freezing or partial freezing of body tissue.

Symptoms: Loss of feeling, discoloration, usually in extremities and face.

Treatment: Warm frost-nipped or superficially frostbitten area with body heat or chemical hand or foot warmers. Protect from more heat loss by adding clothing layers. Eat and drink fluids to encourage blood circulation. Do not rub or massage the area, which can cause permanent damage. If tissue is deeply frozen, do not attempt to rewarm it, which can also cause permanent damage if it refreezes. Instead, protect the area and seek emergency assistance.

BODILY INJURIES

Sprains

Cause: Overextension of limbs, twisting of joints, trauma from an external force or caused by a fall.

Symptoms: Pain, discoloration, distortion, or swelling of affected area.

Treatment: Rest, ice, compression, and elevation (RICE). Sit down and apply a cold pack or wet cloth. Wrap the swollen area and keep it raised above the heart with a sling, if possible. If the person cannot continue on their own, evacuate or call for help.

Open Cuts and Wounds

Cause: Open cuts and wounds can be caused by scrapes from branches, rocks, or gear, and from a fall.

Symptoms: Visible appearance of an open cut or wound and bleeding.

Treatment: With a clean cloth, bandage, gauze, or glove, apply manual pressure for five to ten minutes to stop the bleeding. Raise the injured area above the heart, if you can. Apply more gauze to absorb blood and wrap in a pressure bandage—tightly enough to maintain pressure on the open area, but not so tight that it restricts blood flow. Leave the bandage in place and evacuate or get help.

Concussion

Cause: Head trauma from a strike from an object or from a fall.

Symptoms: Dizziness, blurred vision, loss of consciousness, nausea.

Treatment: Evacuate or get emergency medical help. See a doctor.

BITES, STINGS, AND OTHER POISONS

Poisonous Plants

Cause: Contact with poison ivy, sumac, or oak.

Symptoms: Red skin rash with pain, burning, itching, swelling, or blisters.

Treatment: Wash immediately with soap and cool water to remove the plant oil (urushiol) before it penetrates the skin. Apply calamine lotion or hydrocortisone cream to relieve itching. See a doctor if symptoms persist.

Snakebite

Cause: Bite from a snake.

Symptoms: Puncture wound, pain, swelling.

Treatment: Keep calm, rest, and keep the injured area below heart level. Drink fluids to prevent shock. If you suspect the snake is poisonous, call for emergency help. If you do not and there are no symptoms after twenty minutes of rest, hike out and see a doctor.

Bee and Wasp Stings and Tick Bites

Cause: Sting or bite from a wasp, bee, or tick.

Symptoms: Puncture marks, pain, swelling, stinging or burning sensation, insect attached to skin.

Treatment: If the bee leaves a sack behind, scrape it off quickly. Treat with an oral antihistamine. If the person is allergic, find out if they have epinephrine or other meds in their pack and follow the instructions. For tick bites, remove the tick with fine- or angle-tipped tweezers for slipping between the tick and skin. Grasp the tick as close to the skin as possible and slowly pull straight up—do not twist or tear apart the tick. Clean the area with soap and water or rubbing alcohol, then apply topical triple antibiotic ointment. If you are bitten by a tick, be aware of the signs of bacterial infection such as a rash, fatigue, fever, headache, muscle and joint pain, and joint swelling. This is especially important in areas such as the East Coast, where tick-borne infections like Lyme disease are more common. If you experience any of these symptoms, see your doctor.

Gastrointestinal Illness

Cause: Contaminated food or water.

Symptoms: Stomach pain, cramps, nausea, diarrhea.

Treatment: Replace fluids to prevent dehydration. If symptoms persist, evacuate or get help.

Teresa Gergen pauses on a ledge on her way to the summit of her final US 13er, Palisade Crest in California's John Muir Wilderness. Alyson Kirk is below.
PHOTO BY ADAM MCFARREN

TERESA GERGEN began mountaineering in her late thirties and has climbed most of her peaks solo. Despite illnesses like exercise-induced asthma and injuries including a shattered leg, she has summited more than four thousand peaks in the United States and abroad and is still going. Teresa has stood atop every state highpoint and was the first person to climb every peak over 10,000 feet in Colorado. She is the only person to summit every peak above 13,000 feet—846 13ers and 14ers—in the contiguous United States and Hawaii. Whether she's climbing a mountain alone or with friends, Teresa knows how to set goals and achieve them. She says, "Figure out what motivates you, get some training, make a plan, go get it done. Life's too short to wait."

MISCELLANEOUS INJURIES AND ILLNESSES

Nosebleed

Cause: Trauma, dry air, altitude.

Symptoms: Blood coming out of the nose.

Treatment: Tilt head slightly forward and spit out any blood that drains into your mouth. Pinch nostrils together just below the bony part of the bridge and apply gentle pressure toward your face for five minutes. If the bleeding continues, evacuate or get help.

Lightning Strike

Cause: Being struck by lightning directly, through splash-over from another object that's been struck, or through ground current, water, or other terrain.

Symptoms: Loss of hearing or sight, burns, trauma from being thrown in the air or to the ground, stopped heartbeat (cardiac arrest), and stopped breathing.

Treatment: If there is no breathing or heartbeat, administer CPR and seek emergency assistance.

Panic Attacks

Cause: Reaction to a threat or perceived threat.

Symptoms: Rapid breathing, shaking, nausea, headache, dizziness, being unable to move.

Treatment: Stay calm. Talk through the threat and discuss a plan for getting past it. Fast, heavy breathing can lead to hyperventilation, so have the person breathe into a bag until their breath slows. If a bag isn't handy, get them to make eye contact with you and follow *your* slow, deep, steady breathing. Once the threat has passed, rest and regain composure before continuing.

TAKE STEPS

1. Start building a first-aid kit.
2. Sign up for a CPR or first-aid course.
3. If you are guiding others in the wilderness, take a Wilderness First-Aid course and consider a Wilderness First Responder (WFR) course. National Outdoor Leadership School (NOLS) and other groups offer certifications and refresher certifications.

A group of women get an early start on a hike toward the southwest ridge of La Plata Peak in Colorado's Chaffee County.
PHOTO BY OTINA FOX

PUSHING OFF

At Titcomb Basin in Wyoming's Wind River Range, Jim Rickard and Teresa Gergen study maps in preparation for the route ahead.
PHOTO BY ADAM MCFARREN

CHAPTER 11

LAND NAVIGATION

GETTING FROM trailhead to trailhead without getting lost is a skill many hikers neglect. Instead, they join a group and follow the hike leader, or they rely on a friend with good route-finding skills to show them the way. While convenient, relying on someone else for land navigation means trusting them with your safety—maybe your life. You're also missing out on an opportunity to become more self-sufficient and helpful to others in your hiking group. Land navigation isn't as complicated as it seems. Learn the tools and methods and get some practice. You'll be on your way to becoming a competent land navigator and route finder.

TRAIL NAVIGATION

The simplest form of land navigation is following a trail. If you're hiking in an area with a well-defined trail system, that may be all you need to do. Before your trip, check the land area's website for hike descriptions and information about how long each hike is, how much elevation gain is involved, and whether it's an easy, moderate, or difficult hike. Look for directions to the trailhead and print them out or save them to your phone. Once you've picked out a hike you like, identify the names of the parking area, trailhead, and trails you'll take on your hike. At the trailhead, read the kiosk for information on trail closures, group size limits, fire bans, and animals to be aware of such potential threats as rattlesnakes, mountain lions, and bears. Review the kiosk's map and take notes on where you're going. Then take two pictures of the kiosk map—one of the whole area, and a second zoomed-in shot of the trails you're hiking—so you can refer to them if you need to. Some parking areas have more than one trailhead, or more than one trail at each trailhead, so make sure you start from the right trailhead and get on the right trail. From there, it's just a matter of staying on the trail and stopping at each trail junction to read the trail signs or checking your notes or map to stay on the right path.

MAP NAVIGATION

Maps give you a bird's-eye view of an area so you can see where you are, where you're going, and how to get there. Though some women rely on a GPS or phone app for navigation, these devices depend on battery power and sometimes a good signal to work properly. Rain and cold weather can also affect their performance. A paper map in a plastic bag doesn't need batteries and is immune to weather and reception issues. If you're new to maps, start by learning to read simple trail maps. Before your trip, check the land area's website and see if there's a trail map that you can download to carry with you on your hike. If you're visiting a fee area like a state or national park, you can usually get a map at the pay station or visitor center.

Trails, trailheads, parking areas, restrooms, campsites, and natural features like lakes and mountains are usually labeled or noted with color coding or symbols. Some maps even show the distances of each trail segment. Trail maps are not always oriented with north at the top. Look for a compass on the map so you know where north, south, east, and west are. Also look for a scale on the map showing you the ratio of what's depicted on the map compared to the real world. The scale is usually accompanied by a graphic scale or ruler with distances such as 0.25 mile, 0.5 mile, and 1 mile.

Topo Maps

Topographical maps (or "topos)" provide a three-dimensional view of an area. They are usually oriented with north at the top. The topography of the area—the physical contours of the land, such as hills, valleys, canyons, and mountains—is represented by contour lines. The space between each line represents a set number of feet of elevation above or below sea level. The dark lines are called index lines and are labeled with the elevation of the contour. The thinner, interval lines are not labeled. On some maps, contour lines represent a 40-foot difference in elevation and the distance from one index line to the next is five intervals, or 200 feet. This is not true of every map, so you'll want to find out what each contour line means on your map.

On all topos, the closer the contour lines, the steeper the terrain. Keep in mind that contour maps don't show every single variation in elevation. You could have two consecutive contour lines that appear to show a gentle rise in elevation, but a deep gorge or rocky prominence exists between the two; it just doesn't have a corresponding contour line, so you won't know it's there until you reach it. For the most part, though, topo maps are reliable indicators of topography. They also show vegetation, lakes, waterways, and other terrain.

Standard USGS topo maps cover a 7.5-minute quadrangle of the Earth's surface—⅛ of a degree of latitude by ⅛ of a degree of longitude—and are called 7.5 series maps. Each one is named for a natural feature or a man-made landmark within the quad. If you have a colored map, you have even more information about an area (e.g., water features are blue, and forests are green). If your map has a key, you may be able to identify other features by color or symbol.

Elevation Maps

Elevation maps or profiles show a cross section of the route, usually from trailhead to trailhead, but sometimes only from trailhead to destination. They're particularly useful if you're hiking up a mountain or down into a canyon. You can see the starting elevation and the highpoint or low point to get an estimate of the net elevation gain of the hike, which gives you a general idea of how long it will take to complete it. You can estimate the steepness, too, which helps to determine the difficulty. You can also see all the elevation increases and decreases along the route, which can add more overall elevation, more difficulty, and more time to your hike.

If you're doing a 4-mile round-trip hike (2 miles up and 2 miles back) from 7,000 feet to 9,000 feet, and the elevation map shows a steady rise from trailhead to destination, you will be gaining about 1,000 feet per mile at a roughly 20 percent grade. However, if the elevation profile shows the first mile of the hike as relatively flat, you will have to gain all 2,000 feet in the second mile at a 40 percent grade—twice as steep! That first mile will go fast, but the second one will be much more difficult and take more time. If that same map shows a 500-foot drop in elevation along the route, say, into a deep gully, you will have to regain that elevation on the way up and again on the way out—adding another 1,000 feet of elevation overall to your hike. This information helps you gauge the difficulty of the hike and the time it will take to complete it. You can figure this out with a topo map, but it's easier and more obvious on an elevation profile map.

Using a Map

Before you go on a hike, get the latest map of the area. Visit the land area's website and look for maps that you can download and print, or get a guidebook of the area that includes maps. You can purchase National Geographic *Trails Illustrated* maps from your local outdoor retailer or bookseller or order them online. You can also print out individual quadrangles from the USGS site or ask your local retailer if they can print a map for you. On the map, locate the trailhead where you're starting your hike. If you're doing a loop hike, identify the route—the trail or trails—on the map. For a destination hike, locate your destination and the trail or trails out and back. Pay attention to any trail junctions and natural features on the map.

Ideally, print out an 8½-by-11-inch (or larger) map that covers the entire route. You might keep your *Trails Illustrated* map in your pack, but this printout, sealed in a gallon-size plastic bag and tucked into a pocket of your pants or jacket, is the one you'll refer to most often on the hike. Have a pen or pencil handy to mark your location on the map at regular intervals. *Orientation*—orienting your position on the map—is the first and most important skill you can learn on your way to becoming a good route finder. As you locate your position on a map, put an X on it. You can number your Xs and add the time if you like to keep track of your progress throughout the day. This way, you'll have an estimate of how long it takes you to hike from one point to the next, and you'll be able to estimate how long it will take to hike back out. This is also good information for deciding whether your predetermined turnaround time is still feasible.

While you hike, look for these clues in the field and locate them on the map to orient yourself:

Trail junctions: This is the easiest way to know where you are on a map. When you come to a junction, locate it on the map.

Trail direction: Pay attention to switchbacks on the trail—a change in trail direction—and locate them on the map. Minor switchbacks may not appear on the map, but pronounced shifts in direction are usually apparent.

Natural features and landmarks: Lakes, streams, and mountains, for example.

Trail distance: Over time, you'll have a good idea of how far you hike within a certain time. Use the scale on the map to figure out how far along you are on the trail. For example, if you think you've hiked a mile, measure a mile on the map's scale, then measure that same distance on the map's trail. Use your fingers, a straight edge, or a piece of string as your measuring device. This is not exact, but it gives you a general idea of where you are on a trail.

Elevation: If you have an altimeter or GPS, check the altitude, then find where the trail crosses that elevation on the map. If you don't have an altimeter, you may be able to estimate your elevation by looking for features with known elevations, such as lakes, mountains, or tree line.

Topography: Whenever the topography of your route or the land near your route changes, try to identify that same change on your map. Heading into or out of a canyon, going from level ground to an uphill or downhill section, and sidling up alongside a mountain are good times to look at your map and mark your location. A ridge or gully on the ground appears as a U or V shape of contour lines. If the inner lines have a higher elevation, the U or V is a ridge. If they have a lower elevation than the outer lines, the U or V is a valley, gully, or canyon. A circular contour line surrounded by concentric circles is a summit or a bowl.

Ideally, you should carry a map on any hike where the trail isn't clearly marked from trailhead to trailhead. Even if it is, getting used to using a map on easy trails prepares you for route finding in difficult areas.

COMPASS NAVIGATION

A compass shows you which way is north, south, east, and west. A basic compass is simply a free-floating magnetic needle contained in a round bezel marked with the four cardinal bearings. A *baseplate compass* has other features and can also be used to take *bearings* so you can figure out where you are and plot your destination. For navigation, get a baseplate compass.

The bezel is surrounded by a dial marked in degree increments: 360 total, for the 360 degrees of a circle. Imagine you are standing at the center of the compass. If you turn around in place, what you see is represented by the degrees on the compass. If you face north, you are looking at 0 degrees north. From this position, if you slowly turn a quarter of the way clockwise, you will face from 0 degrees north to 90 degrees east, and everything between is north-northeast (NNE), northeast (NE), or northeast-east (NEE). If you turn another quarter to face backwards, during your rotation you will face from 90 degrees east to 180 degrees south, and everything between is east-southeast, southeast, or south-southeast. Another quarter-turn takes you to 270 degrees due west, and with a final quarter-turn, you are again facing north, at 0 degrees. This is why bearings from 0 to 90 are north to east, from 90 to 180 are east to south, from 180 to 270 are south to west, and from 270 to 360 (or 0) are west to north.

Make sure the compass has an adjustable declination arrow. The short explanation of *declination* and why it matters is this: Earth's magnetic north pole (*geomagnetic north*) is slightly offset from the "top" of the Earth, where the lines of latitude meet (*geographic north*)—at the top of a globe, for example. So while the compass needle swings to magnetic north, it is not pointing in the exact direction that is shown as north on your map. The difference between the two is called the declination, and it varies depending on where you are geographically located. Geomagnetic north moves over time. For this reason, you should mark geographic (or "true") north on your compass before you use it and readjust it as needed every season, or at least annually. Buy a compass with adjustable declination, find out what the declination is for your location,

Maps and a compass are a woman's best friends in the backcountry.

and follow the directions that come with the compass, or check the manufacturer's website to set it. To determine the correct declination (variation from magnetic north), use the calculator on the National Oceanic and Atmospheric Administration (NOAA) site. If you travel to a different region of the country or the world, you will need to adjust it again for the area. The new marking on your compass designating true north is called the *declination arrow* and is the arrow you should use for orientation and land navigation (ignore the north arrow that was originally marked on the compass).

Because the Earth is curved, a rectangular map does not represent with 100 percent accuracy the area on the ground. This is another variation in addition to north declination, but most maps cover such a small area relative to the Earth's surface that the difference is negligible.

Taking a Compass Bearing in the Field

You can't always see your destination from the trailhead, but if you can, take a bearing with your compass. For example, if you're hiking to a mountain and have a clear view of the summit, take a bearing. Stand facing the mountain and hold the compass in front of you at waist level with the baseplate's direction-of-travel arrow pointing toward the summit. Keep the compass level to the ground; don't tilt it up or down. Rotate the bezel to align the eye of the floating needle with the declination arrow that you set, signifying north. Read the number on the bezel at the index line—the line on the baseplate that runs from the direction-of-travel arrow to the bezel. This tells you the bearing (or *azimuth*) from trailhead to summit. Jot down this bearing on the back of your map and label it "Trailhead to Summit." This way, you will have a general bearing to follow on your way to the top.

Now note the number directly *opposite* the bearing. If your bearing is 50 degrees northeast (50° NE), for example, the number opposite 50 is 230, or 230 southwest (230° SW). This is the *back azimuth*, which is always 180 degrees more or less than your bearing. Write the back azimuth on your map and label it "Summit to Trailhead." Now, when you're on the top, you can set your compass to the back azimuth and know immediately the direction to the trailhead. This doesn't mean you just take a direct route on the bearing; you also have to consider trails, terrain, topography, and slope. But knowing the bearing keeps you going in the right direction.

To follow a bearing, again hold the compass at waist height. Turn the bezel to line up the bearing you want to follow with the direction-of-travel arrow. Turn the compass—the *entire* compass, including the baseplate—to line the magnetic needle up with declination north on the bezel. The direction-of-travel arrow is pointing in the direction you need to follow.

MAP AND COMPASS ORIENTATION AND NAVIGATION

A map is useful only if you can match its image to your surroundings. For starters, you have to know which way is north in the backcountry so you can orient your map the same way. Use your compass to orient your map.

A compass can also show you where you are on a map (orientation) and how to get from "Point A" to "Point B" on a map (navigation). This is accomplished by either taking a field bearing and aligning it to the map or vice versa.

To figure out where you are, you will need to have a feature within sight, like a trail junction, lake, or mountain. By taking a bearing with your compass, and then establishing that same bearing on the map, you'll have a good idea of your location on the map. Likewise, if you take a bearing from your current location on a map to a place you want to go, you can set that same bearing and follow your compass to get there. This sounds confusing, but with a little practice it will make sense.

How to Plot Your Location with a Map and Compass (Orientation)

> Similar to the instructions for compass navigation, identify a feature that's within sight and take a bearing with your compass. Point the direction-of-travel arrow toward the feature and rotate the bezel to align the magnetic needle and declination arrow.

> The number that aligns with the index line and direction-of-travel arrow is the bearing between your location and the feature. Knowing this bearing, you can figure out, along a straight line, about where you are on the map.

> Lay your map flat on the ground and place the compass on it with the map's and the bezel's north pointed in the same direction. You are using the compass as a protractor, so ignore the magnetic needle. It doesn't matter which way your map or the needle are facing, as long as they are both oriented in the same direction.

- Locate the known feature on your map. Making sure the bearing you took is still aligned with the compass's index line, put either one of the long straight edges of the compass alongside the feature.
- Without moving the compass edge away from the feature, turn the entire compass (including the baseplate) until the parallel lines inside the bezel, the meridian lines, are parallel with the north-to-south lines on your map.
- You are located somewhere along the line of the baseplate that's touching the feature. Depending on how long the baseplate is, your location could be beyond the line, but it will be in line with the edge of the baseplate. At this point, you may want to draw a line on the map along the compass edge, or just use a piece of string. Extend the line if you need to.
- Since you don't know the distance between yourself and the feature, you can't identify your exact spot with this information. However, you can look for other identifying features from your surroundings that match up with those located along the line you drew on the map to narrow it down. Are you standing on a trail? You are wherever the line crosses the trail on the map. Are you on a ridge? You are standing where the line crosses the ridge.

How to Plot Your Destination with a Map and Compass (Navigation)

- Navigation is similar to the steps you just learned for orientation but followed in the opposite order. First, find your current location and your desired destination on the map.
- Next, lay your compass on the map with one of the longer sides touching your location and your destination. Make sure the direction-of-travel arrow is pointing from your location toward the destination and not the other way around. If the two points are farther apart than the length of the baseplate, again, draw a line or use a piece of string to extend the line.
- Without moving the compass edge away from the two spots on the map, rotate the bezel only (not the baseplate) until the meridian lines are parallel with the north-to-south lines on the map. Check to make sure the declination arrow on your compass is

facing toward north on your map and not south. If it's pointed in the wrong direction, rotate the bezel until it's facing north and the meridian lines are parallel with the north-to-south map lines.

> The number that appears at the index line is the bearing from your location to your destination. Write it down. Now you can use what you learned in the compass navigation paragraphs (above) to hike in the right direction: Hold the compass at waist height. The bearing you took should still be lined up with the index line and direction-of-travel arrow. Turn the compass—the *entire* compass, including the baseplate—to line up the magnetic needle with declination north on the bezel. The direction-of-travel arrow is pointing in the direction you need to follow.

By combining orientation and navigation, you can figure out where you are and how to get where you want to go with very little information other than your map, compass, and a single known feature that you can see and identify in the field and on your map. This skill, known as *orienteering*, isn't difficult, but it takes practice to remember the steps, put them to use, and evaluate the outcome. Like most backcountry skills, the more you use your map and compass, the easier it will be to remember how they work. Then they'll be second nature when you need them.

Other Compass Features

If your compass has a small ruler along one edge, you can use it to compare distances on your map's scale with distances along your route on the map to see how far you've traveled. You can also use it to measure the distance "as the crow flies" (in a straight line) from your current location to your destination. If the compass has a magnifying bubble, you can get a closer look at tiny markings on the map, and if it has a clinometer, you can use that to estimate the slope of a hill. Some compasses have a sighting mirror, which makes orientation even more precise. When you purchase your compass, read the instructions that come with it and visit the manufacturer's website so you can take full advantage of its features.

NAVIGATION WITH ELECTRONICS

Navigation with a GPS or cell-phone app isn't a replacement for map and compass skills. However, for many people electronic navigation tools are convenient and can be easier to learn. Phone apps like Gaia GPS, AllTrails, and Maps 3D PRO give you a two- or three-dimensional view of the area and gobs of information. Every app is different, so before you buy, make sure it works on your phone, whether you have an iOS or Android operating system, and that it's downloadable so you don't have to have cell service to use it in the backcountry. And remember that if your phone runs out of battery power, you won't be able to use the app. If you are going to depend solely on electronics, which is *not* recommended, at least have extra batteries and a solar charger.

An altimeter is a useful device for identifying your altitude. This information makes it easier to identify your location on a topo map, where the elevations are marked. Altimeters are usually included in phone apps and GPS units.

A GPS is a portable battery-powered device that helps you navigate by a global positioning system. In short, the GPS gets information from satellites that you can use to find your way in the backcountry. With a GPS, you can mark waypoints that designate a certain location and create tracks of sequential waypoints that represent a path taken, or to be followed. Waypoints, or coordinates, are expressed in longitude and latitude. You might remember longitude and latitude from grade school, but in case you need a refresher, here it is:

> Latitude represents locations on Earth *north and south* from 0 to +90 north and –90 south. Zero degrees latitude is located at the equator. The total number of latitudinal degrees is 180 from North Pole to South Pole. On a globe, the horizontal lines represent latitude.

> Longitude represents locations on Earth *east and west* from 0 to +180 east and from 0 to –180 west. Zero degrees longitude is located at Greenwich, England, and referred to as "Prime Meridian." The total number of longitudinal degrees is 360, circling the globe. If you look at an actual globe, the vertical lines running from pole to pole represent longitude.

> Each interval of latitude and longitude is called a degree. Each degree is divided into 60 minutes and each minute is divided into 60 seconds. These are not time-related; they are distances.

> A combination of the latitudinal and longitudinal degrees, minutes, and seconds of any place on Earth makes it possible to locate that place on a map as long as the map covers the area where the coordinates are located.

> A waypoint is a series of numbers that represents latitude and longitude. For example, the waypoint (or coordinate) "41.362551, –71.824442" refers to a point on Earth that is 41.362551 degrees north of the equator and 71.824442 degrees west of prime meridian. In the United States, the negative sign is not always used—it's just assumed that longitude is a negative number because the country is entirely located west of 0 longitude.

GPS coordinates may be notated in three different ways:

> Decimal degrees: The positive or negative coordinate represented by (1) the degrees as an integer followed by (2) a decimal point and (3) minutes and seconds as a decimal fraction of a degree. Format: dd.dddd°

> Degrees, decimal minutes: The positive or negative coordinate represented by (1) the degrees as an integer followed by (2) a space with (3) minutes as an integer followed by (4) a decimal point and (5) seconds as a decimal fraction of a minute. Format: –d° mm.mmm'

> Degrees, minutes, seconds: The positive or negative coordinate represented by the degrees, minutes, and seconds as integers separated by spaces. Seconds may appear in decimal form. Format: ddd° mm' s.sss"

How you notate them isn't important, as long as you understand what they mean. If you prefer one format over another, you can set your GPS to use that notation in the Setup menu.

UTM

The Universal Transverse Mercator (UTM) system is another option for referencing waypoints. On a UTM map, vertical and horizontal grid lines (*northings* and *eastings*, respectively) are 1,000 meters apart, or a little over half a mile. In contrast, degrees of latitude and longitude are 2 to 3 miles apart. Northings represent intervals of 1,000 meters north and south of the equator, whereas eastings are 1,000-meter intervals from a reference line that varies depending on the map. UTM coordinates can usually be entered into a GPS through the Setup, Position Format menu. However, before you start experimenting with different position formats, get a thorough understanding of how they work.

YOUR GPS

GPS units have a variety of features and functions, and a thorough explanation of how a GPS works is beyond the scope of this book. If you have one, the quickest way to learn how to use it is to have someone teach you in the backcountry or to take a class.

Learn the basic terminology and common uses of a GPS first. Then practice your GPS skills, and as you get more comfortable with it, learn how other features work. Just knowing how to create and follow waypoints, routes, and tracks can go a long way toward preventing you from getting lost. Following is a list of the basics to learn about your GPS:

› How to turn it on and off, check for battery power, and replace the batteries. If you use your GPS often, use rechargeable NiMH batteries and a battery charger.
› How to locate the various menus. Know how to find the ones you use most often, such as the compass, the altimeter, the trip computer, and the waypoint and track managers.
› How to calibrate the compass in your GPS. Do this every time you change the batteries or start a hike.
› How to clear the track. As long as your GPS is turned on, it's creating a track, or series of waypoints. Clearing the track at the trailhead ensures a clean track.
› How to reset the trip computer.
› How to take and follow waypoints in the backcountry.
› How to create, save, and follow a track and a reverse one.
› How to upload routes, tracks, and waypoints from an online source or a map you made yourself to your GPS, how to view them on your GPS, and how to follow them.
› How to save and download new tracks and waypoints you create from your GPS to a computer or mapping software program.
› How to calibrate the altimeter.
› How to upload maps to the GPS and view them.

Once you get a handle on how to use your GPS, you can upload premade digital maps to it from online sources and map-making apps. If you make your own maps with one of these resources, you can create waypoints and routes to destinations you want to visit, upload them to your GPS, and use them to navigate in the field.

OFF-TRAIL ROUTE FINDING

Not all adventures have trails. Some follow overgrown or snow-packed trails, follow trails only partway, or are completely off-trail. Off-trail route-finding skills help you to navigate in these situations or when you accidentally get off-trail and need to find your way back.

More preparation is necessary for off-trail travel. Your map is not going to show you the route—you have to figure that out for yourself. Research the area. Visit the land area's website, check out online hiking forums for route descriptions and conditions, and read guidebooks and trip reports. Get a topo map or create one with map-making software. Note features like ridges, peaks, valleys, lakes, streams, and vegetation.

If you find a route or track from a reliable online source, see if it makes sense for what you want to do. Upload it to your own mapping software or favorite online mapping site like *CalTopo* or *GPS Visualizer* and tweak it to match your preferred starting point and destination. Or create your own route and waypoints with software or an online site and upload them to your GPS or phone app. Buy or print a map and mark the route and waypoints on it. How much time and effort you put into researching and plotting the route depends on the area. If it's all flat, public land, on easy terrain, there is not much to do. But if you're traveling over mountains and across gullies, avoiding private property and crossing boulder fields, you have work to do.

The Path of Least Resistance

A rule of thumb when planning a route is to take the path of least resistance. Use trails whenever possible. Take established routes and avoid shortcuts. A shorter route on untested terrain may take much longer to follow than a longer route on proven ground. Shortcuts can also put you on difficult or dangerous terrain.

If you travel off-trail, consider the time and effort it will take to pursue your route. If the direct route up a mountain is a steep slope, hike to a saddle to the left or right of it and take the gentler slope to the summit. If there is no saddle, follow the contours of the mountainside, creating left-to-right switchbacks and increasing your elevation to ascend the slope. Avoid losing elevation that you will have to regain or gaining elevation that you will have to lose and regain. Chapter 12 on "Terrain" and chapter 14, "Backcountry Code of Conduct," have more information about choosing a route that's both safe for you and sustainable for the land.

Use Your Map and Compass Skills

Don't neglect your map and compass skills in your planning. Look at your map and identify landmarks that your path will cross. Take bearings between them and mark them on your map, or just make a list of them on the back of your map. This is a lot easier to do at home than it is in the field, and you can then refer to the bearings in the field as you need them. Planning the route is the first step, but the real world looks different than a map. The more off-trail land navigation you do, the more quickly you'll be able to correlate land features and topography between your map and the field, a critical route-finding skill.

Study the Topography

Learn how to read a topo map. The contour lines tell you a lot about a land area's topography so you can quickly identify features when you see them in the backcountry. If you have an altimeter, you can compare the elevation on your altimeter in the field with the contour lines near your location on the map to get a better idea of where you are.

Use Intermediate Objectives to Get to Your Destination

In the field, try to eyeball intermediate objectives that are in your line of sight or on the same bearing between you and your destination. Hike to the objective, then identify another objective between yourself and your destination. Breaking your hike up into sections like this is easier than trying to stay on a bearing for miles, working around numerous obstructions.

Verify Waypoints and Make New Ones

If you uploaded waypoints to a GPS and are following them, verify that they are correct along your hike. If they are not, make a new waypoint for the actual spot you were trying to locate. Make new waypoints for any other identifiable locations like trail junctions, clearings, stream crossings, and summits.

Pay Attention to Trail Junctions

Trail junctions may seem obvious heading toward a destination but can be confusing when you're headed in the other direction. Make a waypoint or take a note so you don't forget which way to go to get back to the trailhead. Sometimes trail junctions aren't obvious at all because the connecting trail forks backward from the trail you're on. You can walk right past these junctions without noticing them, but when you're coming back and headed in the opposite direction, they clearly appear as a fork in the trail. Unless you've noted them, you may not know which fork to take.

Look for Base Lines and Handrails

Base lines and handrails are long, man-made, or naturally occurring features in the backcountry that are helpful in land navigation. A road, trail, river, railroad tracks, cliff edge, or mountain ridge can be used as a base line or handrail.

The difference between the two is how they are used. A base line is a feature you hike to and follow to get to a destination. Think of a road or a river that leads to the trailhead, or close to the trailhead. A handrail is a feature that you use as a guide. You don't necessarily follow it, but you know that as long as you don't cross it, you're on the right track. If there's a river west of your route and a mountain east of your route, you know that as long as you don't cross the river or climb over the mountain, you're generally on track. Of course, you could overshoot your destination, so you need to pay attention to the distance and topography and use your map and compass skills.

Identify potential base lines and handrails during the planning stage of your hike. Be aware of any that appear during your hike, too. Not everything is shown on a map. New roads and trails are built, and rivers can become diverted and create streams where you don't expect them.

Use Offsetting (or Offshooting)

If you know the distance and the general direction to a location but are worried that you may not be able to reach the exact spot, take a direction that leads you to the left or to the right of the destination. Once you have traveled a distance slightly farther than you think the destination is located, turn left (if you traveled to the right of it) or right (if you traveled to the left of it). Without intentional offsetting, you could end up on either side of your destination with no way of knowing which way to turn to reach it.

Pay Attention Anytime the Direction or the Terrain Changes

If you are hiking through a forest and come out into a clearing, make note of your exit point. Take a waypoint or build a temporary cairn from rocks so you can find your way to that same point on the way back. Dismantle the cairn on your way out. Use the same method for marking stream crossings, talus and boulder field exits, and switchbacks. These changes in direction or terrain may seem obvious in the light of the morning when your mind's sharp and you're full of energy, but they can be easy to miss in failing light, when you're tired.

Tracking your location on a map is a good habit to get into on any hike, but it's especially crucial when you're not on a defined trail. If you feel like you're off-track, return to your last known location and figure out the correct route, look for handrails to help you get back on track, or hike to the nearest base line and return to the trailhead.

TAKE STEPS

1. Get a compass and plan your next hike on a map. Take bearings from trailhead to destination and vice versa and write the azimuth and back azimuth on the map. Test them out in the field.
2. Take a map and compass land navigation class that includes field work.
3. Get a GPS or find a phone app you like and learn how to use them.

Windstorms, landslides, avalanches, and other natural events can turn a groomed trail into a maze of deadfall and debris. Lisa Heckel scrambles between fallen tree trunks on the Ruby Creek approach to Turret Peak, her final Colorado Centennials summit.
PHOTO BY TIMOTHY HECKEL

CHAPTER 12

TERRAIN

KNOWING THE TYPE of terrain your route crosses informs the skills and gear you need. This comes in handy when you're planning a route, estimating how long it will take, and packing food, drinks, gear, and clothing. For example, a snowfield may be much easier to cross than a boulder field, so you'll make better time. However, you may want to pack snowshoes and gaiters. Or maybe there are a lot of streams to cross on your route, which will add time to your outing. You might want to bring trekking poles and water shoes for the crossings. Since some terrain takes longer to navigate, you could be out later than expected. You could decide to pack more food, an extra headlamp, and more batteries for your GPS. There is no rule or formula for calculating how long it takes to cross different types of terrain. The more you get out there, the better you'll get at estimating your typical progress.

Established trails: Trails provide safe, sustainable access to natural places. They are built to handle a lot of foot traffic with minimal damage to the backcountry. If there's an established trail on your route, use it. Shortcutting trails puts you on more difficult, potentially dangerous terrain and can cause erosion. You will make much better time hiking on trails than off-trail, even if you have to hike farther.

Game trails and social trails: Game trails are created by animals and social trails are created by people hiking off-trail. Though not well-groomed like established trails, game and social trails are easier to navigate than cutting through dense brush. However, you have no way of knowing where the trail leads, so follow with caution. If a social trail is closed off in the backcountry, don't follow it at all. Look for an established trail—which should *always* be your first choice—to reach your destination.

Cryptobiotic (biological crust) soil and tundra: Biological crust soil, found in arid regions, and tundra, found at high altitudes, are fragile soils that play a critical role in the environment. It takes hundreds, sometimes *thousands* of years for this type of soil to form. Don't walk on it. If it's in your path, find a way around it.

Grass: Avoid hiking on grasses. If you must cross a grassy area, look for rocks to step on to avoid damaging plant life. Groups should spread out to avoid hiking the same path on grass. In tall, wet grass, put on a rain jacket and rain pants and check for ticks at your next break.

Deadfall: Fallen trees can take an excruciatingly long time to navigate. Avoid deadfall on your route and go around it if possible. If you have to cross deadfall, carefully go over or under tree trunks and limbs. Avoid standing on deadfall, which can be rotten and collapse under your weight.

A buff and hood protect the author's nose, mouth, and ears from blowing sand at Great Sand Dunes National Park and Preserve in southern Colorado.

Sand dunes: Making progress through sand is slow, especially going uphill. Avoid steep slopes and aim for intermediate objectives on low-angle slopes. Contour the land with switchbacks. For going downhill on sand, you can plunge-step if you are comfortable traveling this way. Just make sure you are not sucked into a sandy pit that you'll have to climb out of.

Hardpan: Hardpan is soil that's packed down. It offers little resistance and can be slippery. On steep hardpan, walk with your feet straight ahead when going downhill for more surface area against the pull of gravity. Look for securely embedded rocks in the dirt for foot placement and more solid purchase. If you have trekking poles, use them.

Scree: Scree is basically large pebbles. A deep, dense layer of scree can be navigated in a similar fashion as sand, avoiding steep slopes on the uphill and plunge-stepping on the descent. Short gaiters are helpful for keeping scree out of your boots.

Scree on hardpan: Loose scree on hard-packed dirt is especially annoying because the granules are like ball bearings under your feet. Take your time on this kind of terrain to avoid slips and twisted ankles. If you're walking with other people, surefooted hikers can take the lead, allowing others to hike slightly behind them, with one hand on the shoulder of the person ahead for balance.

Talus: Football-size rocks tend to have uneven surfaces. They can shift under your weight, and if they're wet, they may be slippery. Hiking over

Established trails avoid steep, loose talus fields like the one on Greenhorn Mountain in Pueblo County, Colorado.

talus takes time and demands your attention. Mid-height boots can help protect your ankles from getting banged up. Some people like to use a pair of trekking poles on talus; others use one pole for balance and have one hand free to catch themselves if they fall; and still others prefer to rock-hop over talus with no poles at all. With practice, you'll figure out what works best for you.

Boulder fields: Boulder fields may require use of both hands and feet. Have at least one hand free, wear boots with grippy soles, and take your time. Test a boulder before you put your weight on it, as they can teeter and shift. Keep an eye on others in your party in a boulder field, especially if the boulders are so large that they could hide a fallen person.

Mud: Avoid hiking muddy trails, which creates ruts and causes permanent trail damage and erosion. If you think you might end up on a muddy trail, wear mid-height boots to keep your socks dry and use trekking poles to maintain your balance. Stay on trail despite the mud, to avoid creating social trails and trail braiding.

Marshes: Hike around marshes if you can, or you'll end up in mud and wet grass. You could put your foot into a deep hole and get soaked or even have your boot sucked off your foot.

Brush: Traveling through dense brush, or "bushwhacking," is sometimes unavoidable. Protect your arms and legs with long pants and a long-sleeved shirt, preferably with smooth fabric that doesn't catch on branches.

Stream crossings: Research your route and if there are stream crossings, find out if bridges exist. If they do, plan your route to take advantage of them. Natural bridges made of tree trunks, limbs, and rocks vary in their

Jean Aschenbrenner carefully makes her way over a log bridge and beaver dam in Colorado's Lost Creek Wilderness en route to Unnamed 10620. PHOTO BY KEN NOLAN

strength and, if wet, can be very slippery. Use trekking poles for balance to get across, and if you don't trust a bridge, consider crossing the stream in your boots. You can even pack a lightweight pair of water shoes or old sneakers for hikes with known stream crossings and no bridges. If you wear water shoes, tie your boots to your pack so you don't accidentally drop them in the water. If you have to cross deep water, try to find a spot where the river is narrowest so you can jump across or shallow enough to wade across. Otherwise, you may have to use a rope as a safety line to get across. Avoid crossing deep or rushing water. If you are not 100 percent certain that you can cross it safely, don't do it. You could lose your life.

Cliffs: Stay away from cliff edges, which may appear solid but could be soft and unable to hold your weight. Cliffs at the tops of waterfalls are especially dangerous because the water current can push you over the edge.

Exposure: Some outings require hiking or scrambling over "exposed" areas where a fall could be fatal. On any exposed area, maintain three points of contact—two hands and a foot or two feet and a hand—on solid rock or ground. Moving across exposed areas is more of a mental challenge than a physical one, and you may have to work up to it. If you're uncomfortable on exposure, rope up. Tie into a rope that's properly anchored so that if you do fall, you won't go far. Roping up is not a skill to learn on the fly; you or someone in your party will need to know how to anchor the rope and tie people into it safely.

Deposition zones: Deposition zones and terrain traps are areas below a slope where rockfall or avalanche debris collects. Avoid these areas, especially if the slope is snow-covered, and after heavy rainfall when rocks can become dislodged and fall.

Ice: Wear spikes or other foot traction on icy trails and use trekking poles for balance. On very steep inclines or hard snow or ice, you may need sturdier, more aggressive traction, like crampons.

Slush and soft or wet snow: Wet snow is best avoided, but if your route takes you through it, wear mid-height waterproof boots and winter gaiters to keep your feet and legs dry. If the snow is soft and deep enough, you could be post-holing, one of the most unpleasant modes of travel. Take turns leading the hike so the person in front can break trail for a certain distance or number of steps. Then, that person goes to the "back of the line" and the next person takes over. This will give everyone a break and prevent burnout.

Firm snow: Firm snow with a solid bootpack from previous hikers can be hiked in boots or with boots and spikes. If there is no bootpack, skis, snowshoes, or boots and winter gaiters may be worn.

Cornices: Cornices are overhanging eaves of snow that form on the leeward side of cliffs and mountain ridges. They can collapse under you or fall on top of you. Never step on a cornice or hike under one.

Snow slopes: Even low-angle snow-packed slopes can avalanche. Chapter 22 in this book, "Winter in the Wilderness," has more information on avalanche safety. As a general rule, on snowy terrain, avoid snow slopes and stick to ridges. The exception is when you are intentionally kick-stepping up a couloir or a snow slope that you know is not in danger of avalanching. If you're going to travel in this kind of territory, get some avalanche safety training.

TAKE STEPS

1. If you're used to hiking only on groomed trails, find a hike that crosses terrain you haven't tried. Start with short, easy sections, and don't go alone.
2. Check out gear that will help you navigate specific terrain at your local outdoor retailer, like trekking poles and boot traction.
3. Pay attention to how much time it takes to cross different terrain. This will help you plan better for future hikes.

Golden aspens signal the
coming fall and changing
weather in the high country.
PHOTO OF THE AUTHOR
BY DOUG HATFIELD

CHAPTER 13

WEATHER

WEATHER CAN HAVE a dramatic effect on your backcountry experience. Sun, wind, fog, and precipitation in the form of rain, sleet, hail, graupel (snow, covered in a layer of ice), and snow not only can impact your hike, but also can make the road to the trailhead impassable and your campsite unlivable. While it's true that you can camp and hike in just about any weather with the right gear and clothing, you may not enjoy it, and you could put yourself in a dangerous situation. Plan ahead, pick weather days that you're prepared to endure, evaluate the weather in the field, know how to spot deteriorating conditions, and turn around before you get into a dangerous situation.

PLAN AHEAD

When you plan a hike, check the forecast for the days you expect to be out there. Pay attention to temperature highs and lows, chance of precipitation, wind speed, and wind direction. Check again in the days leading up to your hike to see if the earlier predictions changed. The National Weather Service site provides current conditions and extended forecasts. Search by zip code or county, or narrow your search to the closest city or a topographic feature, like a lake or a mountain. Check the weather pattern leading up to your hike and right after your hike. If a storm is moving out the day before you hike or moving in the day after, there's a chance the forecast could be off by a day or more, so check to see if the prediction shifts.

PACK FOR THE WORST-CASE FORECAST

If there's a chance of precipitation, make sure you have a hooded raincoat in your pack. If high winds are predicted, pack for high winds—windproof jacket, buff, and in winter above tree line, goggles. Look at how

Jean Aschenbrenner hikes through a whiteout at high altitude on Colorado's Huron Peak. Jean and her partner's familiarity with the peak and route led to their decision to continue, knowing they would have to deal with blowing snow and poor visibility.
PHOTO BY KEN NOLAN

the weather could affect the topography of the area where you're camping and hiking, too. Low areas could get flooded. High areas are more susceptible to winds, and you could have a tougher time finding shelter in bad weather, especially above tree line. Gap winds, funneled through mountain passes, could reach speeds much higher than predicted. Wind in areas of low or no vegetation, like deserts and sand dunes, can whip up debris that impairs visibility. Wear the right clothing, pack the right gear, and be honest with yourself about the types of weather you are physically, mentally, and technically able to endure.

EVALUATE THE WEATHER DURING YOUR HIKE

It's natural to focus on your immediate surroundings when you hike. Avoid weather surprises by making a habit of looking at the sky periodically. The most obvious signs of impending weather are shifts in wind direction or speed, cloud formations, and changes in air pressure. The weather forecast tells you which way the wind is coming from, not which way it's blowing. If the forecast calls for SSW winds at 5 mph, verify that on your hike. Is there a light breeze coming from the south-southwest? If the wind picks up or shifts direction, pay attention. Look for clouds overhead. Clouds aren't necessarily a warning sign, but they can tell you something about impending weather. Clouds are formed when less dense warm air rises, taking moisture with it. The warm air cools and becomes denser, forming clouds. Building clouds, especially clouds that grow vertically, can be a sign of coming precipitation. Darkening cloud bottoms indicate an immediate threat of rain and could signal thunder and lightning. Clouds generally move in the same direction as the wind, so you're in a better position if they're moving away from you. However, you won't know how fast they're moving or whether they're a sign of lightning, so if clouds are building and darkening around you, seek shelter or hike out.

Changes in air pressure can also indicate a change in weather. This is caused by an area of denser air moving into an area of less dense air. You can monitor air pressure changes with a barometer or with an altimeter. Your GPS has a built-in altimeter for gauging elevation. If you don't have a GPS, consider getting a barometer. On an altimeter, elevation appears to increase as barometric pressure decreases, even when you're not actually increasing your elevation. So if the elevation on your GPS is going up but you're not going uphill, you know that a low-pressure system is moving in. Likewise, a decrease in altitude on your GPS while you maintain the same elevation indicates a high-pressure system.

Nothing takes the place of planning ahead and watching the weather throughout the day, but it's not a bad idea to have a weather app with a radar map on your phone so that if you have service, you can check for weather changes throughout the day. Smartphone apps provide radar maps that use the Doppler effect to show current precipitation as color-coded bands in the atmosphere. Precipitation typically follows the same path as prevailing winds, so if you know the wind direction, you can figure out if rain is moving toward you or away from you.

TAKE COVER OR TURN AROUND

No matter how well you prepare for the weather or evaluate it on a hike, you could still end up in a bad situation. Weather forecasts are not 100 percent accurate 100 percent of the time. If you see signs of deteriorating weather that you are not prepared to deal with, decide whether to take cover or turn around. You don't have to beat it back to the trailhead at the first sign of a storm cloud, but use your knowledge and common sense to determine whether continuing is prudent.

Extreme weather—high heat, intense cold, debilitating winds, and monsoon rains that flood low areas and dislodge rocks on slopes—can kill you. So can a lightning strike. Don't wait until you're forced to make a

Otina Fox climbs Crestone Peak to ski the Red Gully. Sunny days can change quickly in the mountains, so she is dressed for the best and prepared for the worst.
PHOTO COURTESY OF OTINA FOX

OTINA FOX is a seismic software engineer, web designer/programmer, ski mountaineer, photographer, hiker, climber, and biker. She has hiked and climbed since she was a teen in Austria, Germany; in the Adirondacks of New York; Alaska; Ireland; and around the western United States, including her home state of Colorado. Otina has battled cold-, allergen-, and exercise-induced asthma since she was a child, and found out in her early thirties that she was celiac, leading to major lifestyle changes. She adopted a paleo diet, focused on reducing stress, and prioritized sleep, changes that had a dramatic positive effect on her health and performance. While skiing Maroon Peak in 2014, she shattered her left leg at 13,000 feet in a freak accident caused by a binding failure. Despite two more leg breaks in four years, she continues to ski and mountaineer. Physical therapy, a personal trainer, and cardio and weight training keep her performing at a high level. Otina organizes and leads women's hiking and ski groups, focusing on inclusive trips into the mountains and backcountry. She posts trip reports of her adventures on sites like 14ers.com and her own site, otinasadventures.com. Otina's goals include skiing all of Colorado's 14ers, hiking the state's 13ers, completing the Colorado Trail, and improving her trad climbing and mountain-biking skills.

quick decision. Monitor the weather and take action while you still have options, like when you're not too far from the trailhead or camp, or when you're near a wooded area instead of stranded in an open field or on the side of a mountain.

Don't take chances with lightning at all. Stay at least 6 miles from a lightning storm. You can tell how far you are from lightning with the flash-to-bang method of timing the seconds between the flash of light and the audible boom that follows. Divide the number of seconds by five to get the distance in miles that you are from the lightning. If you count thirty seconds, you are 6 miles from the storm. If you count fewer than thirty seconds, the storm is less than 6 miles away and you are not safe. You can also use this method to determine whether the storm is moving toward or away from you. You are at higher risk of being struck in a large open area, near a body of water, or high up, at altitude.

A rule of thumb for climbing at altitude, especially during the stormy summer months, is to plan to be off the summit by noon. But if it's eleven a.m. and you can hear thunder, don't continue going up. You will likely end up on the highpoint at the worst possible time. If you're hiking with a group, continue hiking out but spread apart to lessen the odds of more than one person being hit in a strike. That way, if someone is hit, the others can come to the injured person's aid. If the storm is upon you and you have nowhere to go, you may have to wait it out. Fling any metal objects that you're carrying—trekking poles, tent poles, and ice axe—far away. Don't stand up, which allows a ground strike to travel from your feet up to your head, and don't lie down, which puts your whole body in contact with the ground. Crouch down over your pack or on your sleeping pad and cover your ears.

TAKE STEPS

1. Check out the National Weather Service site and locate information on temperatures, wind speed, wind direction, and chance of precipitation for an area. Check a day or two later to see if the forecast has changed.

2. Find a weather app that you like with radar maps and practice using it.

3. On your next outing, make a point to check the sky periodically and note cloud formations. Pay attention to the wind direction, and if you have a barometer, note the changes in air pressure.

The author treads lightly on a rocky scramble over talus and boulders on California's Mount Russell.
PHOTO BY DOUG HATFIELD

CHAPTER 14

BACKCOUNTRY CODE OF CONDUCT

THERE IS NO formal code for how to conduct yourself in the backcountry. There *are* a few general rules that will lessen your impact on the environment and the experiences of others. When in doubt, think about how your actions affect other people and the wild places we all share. Then do the right thing.

Crowds: Limit the size of your group. Some wilderness areas have rules for how many people can travel together.

Be prepared and on time: Respect your hiking partners by preparing and being on time.

Right-of-way on dirt roads: On narrow dirt roads to the trailhead, the driver going uphill has the right-of-way. If you're going downhill, carefully back up and allow the other driver to pass. However, regardless of whether you're going up or down, if there's a pull-out nearby, pull over and let the other driver pass.

Leave No Trace: Leave the places you visit the way you found them, or better. Do not remove rocks, plants, flowers, or artifacts. Do not leave trash or anything else behind, including painted rocks or writings or carvings on trees or rocks. The Leave No Trace website has seven principles for leaving no trace behind.

Noise: Respect wildlife and other backcountry enthusiasts by using your "indoor voice," especially at night. Avoid making cell-phone calls, but if you have to, keep your voice low so other people's wilderness experiences aren't affected.

Dogs: Follow the land area rules for dogs. Some places allow dogs on leash or voice control. In other areas, dogs aren't allowed at all. Don't allow your dog to jump on other hikers, and never allow them to chase wild animals.

Hikers stick to the trail and use rocks to cross a stream, minimizing their impact.
PHOTO BY DARIA HOLLER

Fires: Follow fire restrictions and never leave a fire unattended. If you have a fire, make sure it's put out completely before leaving the campsite.

Right-of-way on the trail: Trail right-of-way is the same as road right-of-way. Downhill hikers should yield to uphill hikers. However, if you're hiking solo and are approached by a group, step off the trail no matter which way you're going and allow the group to pass. On most multi-use trails, bikers should yield to hikers and hikers should yield to horses. This is not always the case, and bikers often act like they have the right-of-way. If you're on a trail popular with mountain bikers, listen for their approach so you don't get run over. Do not wear earbuds or you may not hear them coming.

Stay the trail: If there's a trail, use it. Don't walk along the edges, which causes trail widening or braiding. Don't cut switchbacks, which creates social trails and causes erosion.

Stay off areas that are closed for revegetation: You need time to rest and recover and so does the land. Give it a break.

Trekking poles: Trekking poles assist with balance and take some of the pressure off your joints, but they can also damage the land. Use your poles on the trail and avoid poking holes into the ground outside trail edges. Don't use poles on tundra, biological crust soil, or plant life.

Avoid busy trails: Instead of visiting the busiest parks in your area, look for out-of-the-way places to give busy areas a break.

Avoid trails after heavy rains: Popular dirt trails can become extremely muddy after a heavy rain. Find another place to hike and give them a chance to dry out. Constant foot traffic causes rutting on soggy trails.

Share trail-breaking: If you're slogging through deep snow with other hikers, take turns breaking trail so no one burns out.

Avoid the accordion effect: If people in your hiking group get behind, stop and give them a chance to catch up. Then, instead of immediately taking off, give them a minute or two to catch their breath and consider slowing your pace so they don't keep getting behind.

Don't climb over others: On loose, rocky slopes, don't climb over other hikers and avoid dislodging rocks. If you accidentally kick a rock, yell "Rock!" loudly to warn people below you.

Never throw anything off or down a mountain: It may be hard to believe, but some people make a sport of throwing rocks, hitting golf balls, or tumbling boulders off peaks and down gullies and couloirs. These projectiles could start an avalanche or rockslide, and injure or even kill a person or an animal.

Lost and found: If you find something on the trail that's been dropped by another hiker, carry it to the trailhead and leave it in an obvious place where they can find it. For expensive items like a cell phone or GPS, you may try to locate the person online.

Wildlife: Stay away from animals. Don't approach them, pet them, feed them, or provoke them. Keep a safe distance.

Volunteer: Give back by volunteering for trail work and restoration projects at your favorite areas.

TAKE STEPS

1. On your next hike, be aware of how your behavior affects other people and the environment.
2. If you see trash on the trail—even someone else's trash—pack it out.
3. Check out the Leave No Trace site for more information on backcountry protocol.

Crampons and helmet promote safer climbing for Otina Fox on Maroon Peak's Bell Chord in the Elk Mountains near Aspen, Colorado.
PHOTO COURTESY OF OTINA FOX

CHAPTER 15

PLAYING IT SAFE

EVEN EXPERIENCED, KNOWLEDGEABLE people can make bad decisions in the backcountry. Whether people are lulled into complacency, caught up in the excitement of the moment, or caught off-guard by unexpected situations, mistakes happen. Following best practices will help keep you out of trouble (most of the time), while listening to your inner voice will often clue you in to impending danger. Your senses pick up all kinds of information, and even though it may not make sense to you immediately, your subconscious often sounds the alarm. If your intuition tells you that something doesn't *feel* right, listen to that alarm. Stop and figure it out.

BEFORE YOU LEAVE FOR A TRIP

Have a trip plan, share it, and stick to it. This important step is skipped by the majority of outdoor enthusiasts. If you've never had an emergency in the backcountry that prevented your safe return, sharing a plan seems like wasted effort. The one time you don't do it could be the day that you get into trouble, and if no one knows where you are, a small problem can turn serious. Chapter 19, "Trip Planning," details the specifics to include in your trip plan.

Get an extra key made for your vehicle. People lose keys on the trail. Make sure you have a backup. Stash it in a magnetic key-keeper or give it to someone in your party to hang onto. Getting a locksmith to drive to a remote trailhead will cost you a lot of money.

Have a roadside emergency kit in your car. At the very least, have a spare tire, a car jack, tire iron, and something to serve as a platform to put the car jack on so it won't sink into the dirt or mud when you're changing the tire. In addition to these basics, you can buy an emergency kit or build your own. Add a snow shovel for digging out of drifts, a handsaw for cutting tree branches that block the road to the trailhead, and food, water, a sleeping bag, and blankets in case you get stuck overnight. In snowy conditions, bring snowshoes even if you aren't using them on your hike. If you're stranded, you could have a long hike out.

Practice self-care before your trip. Clip your fingernails and toenails a day or two before your trip, hydrate with water and electrolyte drinks, and eat a healthy meal with enough complex carbohydrates to get you through the next day. If you typically exercise every day, use the day before your hike as a rest day so your legs are fresh for the hike. Get a good night's sleep.

Charge your cell phone and bring an adapter that works with your car's USB, cigarette lighter, or other charging port. You could be out later than expected and will need juice in your phone to let your point of contact know you're safe but running late. However, do not leave the phone plugged in for a long time while the car isn't running, which can drain the battery.

Charge batteries for your GPS, camera, and other electronic devices. Get in the habit of doing this after every hike so you always have fresh batteries.

Gas up the night before you leave for the trailhead. Getting towed from a remote trailhead is also expensive.

Pack the night before your trip, sooner for extended trips. Packing can take longer than you think. Lay out your clothes and prepare your pack. Get your food together and put it in a bag on the top shelf of the fridge so you don't forget it. If you're using a cooler, put it somewhere obvious to remind yourself to pack the food, like in front of your front door or the door to the garage. Late starts can mess with your plans and with your head, and you'll be calmer and more clearheaded if you start on time. If you're not a "morning person," consider camping at the trailhead or nearby campground the night before your hike.

ON THE ROAD

When driving to the trailhead, be aware of changing conditions, especially during inclement weather or natural disasters. Rainfall, snowfall, rockfalls, mudslides, and wildfires can impact your route. Be prepared to turn around if conditions become unsafe.

Watch for runners, bicyclists, motorcyclists, and wildlife on the road. Deer and other animals are especially active along the roadways at dusk and dawn when the lighting is bad and you're on your way to or from the trailhead.

Don't overestimate your ability, or the ability of your vehicle, to make it to a trailhead. When in doubt on a rough road, pull over and park completely off the road—or turn around and drive to a safe place to park—and then walk to the trailhead. Did I mention that tows in the backcountry are expensive?

AT THE TRAILHEAD

Hide valuables in your car or carry them with you. Don't leave purses, wallets, electronics, or gear in view, tempting "smash-and-grab" thieves.

Avoid leaving food in the car. If you're parking in an area that's home to bears, do not leave food in the car. Bears have been known to tear off car doors to get to food, and even if they don't see it, they might smell it. Use a bear locker or carry food with you, especially for multiday hikes.

Check the trailhead kiosk. Look for current notifications such as trail closures, fire restrictions, and animal sightings.

AT CAMP AND ON THE TRAIL

Keep an eye on the weather. Use your eyes, ears, altimeter, and weather app to prevent ending up in bad weather.

Stay off unstable terrain. Loose rocks can pop out of the earth above you and below your feet. Look for the most solid path, especially on steep slopes and near cliff edges.

Follow good orientation and navigation principles to avoid getting lost. Carry a map and compass plus your preferred land navigation tools, such as a GPS or phone app. Track your progress regularly, don't take shortcuts, and if you lose track of where you are and can't identify your location by your surroundings, return to your last known location.

Consider carrying a satellite messenger or **personal locator beacon (PLB)**. Emergency signaling devices like satellite messengers and personal locator beacons don't take the place of education, experience, and sound judgment, but they could save your life.

Jean Aschenbrenner plays it safe on a steep section of Colorado's Crestone Peak by roping up and placing protection ahead of partners Ken Nolan and Dwight Sunwall.
PHOTO BY DWIGHT SUNWALL

> **Satellite messenger devices** require a subscription, but they have valuable features, such as the capacity to send messages to people while you're in the backcountry, much like texting on your phone. You can preprogram messages, too, to let people know whether you're safe or in trouble. These devices also have some navigation functionality, but features vary between brands, so do your homework and compare features, functions, and subscription plans before you buy. Have an extra set of rechargeable batteries and a charger for your satellite messenger, and make sure the batteries are charged before you head into the backcountry.

> **Personal locator beacons (PLBs)** do not require a subscription, but the functionality is limited. They are primarily meant for getting an SOS signal, along with your location, to emergency personnel. Registration is required before you can use your PLB, and you have to send it to the dealer for battery replacement. PLB coverage is wider and the signal is stronger than a satellite messenger.

Pack a shiny emergency blanket or small mirror. These items can double as signaling devices if you need to attract the attention of a rescue plane or helicopter.

Carry a whistle and/or pepper spray. While attacks by other people in the backcountry are rare, they have happened. If you decide to carry a whistle to signal for help or pepper spray to ward off an attacker, clip it to your pack strap where you can get to it immediately.

Don't mess with animals. Small animals can carry serious diseases. Large ones can bite, kick, claw, and trample you. Unprovoked animal attacks are rare. They usually occur when an animal is approached or surprised. Animals in the wild tend to be most active at dawn and dusk. If you are worried about them, here are some tips to stay safe:

> **Bears:** Don't leave food or trash in your tent. Use a bear-proof canister, hang it in a bear bag, or lock it out of sight in a bear locker at the trailhead or campground. If you use a bear bag, follow the instructions and hang it only from live, sturdy trees high enough and far enough from the trunk so the bear can't get to it. If you expect to find bears on the trail, avoid surprising them by talking, whistling softly, or singing so they hear you coming. If you see a bear on the trail, just stop, then slowly back away. Don't run. Some bears will leave you alone if you play dead, but others will attack. Find out if there is a certain type of bear common to the area where you're camping and hiking—black bears, grizzlies, etc.—and research the best way to ward off attacks for that type. If you are going to be spending time in an area where bears have been reported, consider carrying bear spray. Make sure you have it in a place you can get to quickly, like the front of a pack strap, and know how to use it. The bear will not wait while you search through your pack, locate the spray, and read the directions.

> **Mountain lions, cougars, and panthers:** Keep kids and dogs close at hand in areas where wild cats live. Hike in a group, and if you suspect there is a cat nearby, raise your hands over your head to make yourself appear larger. Do not run or the cat may mistake you for prey and follow its instinct to chase and attack.

> **Deer, elk, mountain goats, and bighorn sheep:** Stay away from them and they are not likely to approach you. If they become aggressive, wave your arms and make some noise. Don't stomp your feet or they may take it as a challenge. Protect yourself with your trekking poles if you have to. Goats are attracted to salt and

Bear spray, bear bells, hand and toe warmers, and safety whistles can keep you safe and help you out in emergency situations.

they know it's found in urine. Don't pee in view of a goat, near your tent, or on the trail.

> **Moose:** Moose are more easily provoked than deer or elk. Keep a safe distance and never approach them. If you see one on the trail, back away slowly and get behind a tree. If the moose attacks you, curl up on the ground, protect your head and face, and wait for it to leave.

> **Marmots and pika:** Marmots and pika live in alpine environments. They will chew up anything with salt on it—meaning, any items that may have residue from your sweat or urine. Don't leave items like trekking poles or boots unattended or outside overnight. You can sprinkle coyote urine, sold at garden shops, around your campsite to keep them at bay. If a trailhead has a serious marmot problem, you may have to put chicken wire or plastic snow fencing around the bottom of the car to prevent them from crawling up into the engine and chewing on your car's wiring. Alterna-

tively, use a large tarp. Drive over it to secure the tarp under your front tires and wrap it over the hood.

> **Wolves, foxes, and coyotes:** Attacks on humans are extremely rare. Keep your distance, and if they approach, make some noise, protect yourself, and fight back with whatever you have available, including your feet and your fists.

> **Alligators:** Alligators live near water and in swampy areas. Like most other animals in the wild, they generally want nothing to do with you, but if you surprise them or approach them, they may attack. Avoid hiking in areas where they live, and if you have to cross an area where there are alligators, don't go into the water, and be sure to keep children and pets close by. If you see one, run away fast at a 45-degree angle so the alligator will have to turn its body to chase you. If you get bitten, scream as loud as you can and fight back.

AFTER THE HIKE

Don't drive drowsy. If you get back to the trailhead and you're too tired to drive safely, set the alarm on your phone and take a nap. Call or text your point of contact to let them know you'll be late. If you're rushing home because you have to get to work in the morning, you are better off sleeping an hour or two in your car, driving home, and just getting a couple less hours sleep in your bed. If you get tired on the drive home, pull into a parking lot and sleep.

TAKE STEPS

1. Get an extra key made for your car and decide where to keep it.
2. Start building a roadside emergency kit for your car.
3. Research the areas you're visiting next to find out if there is any known animal activity.

Not all routes have trails. Jean Aschenbrenner navigates the Halo Ridge Route on Mount of the Holy Cross, Colorado.
PHOTO BY KEN NOLAN

REACHING
NEW HEIGHTS

Trail running keeps Alyson Kirk in cardio shape between long-distance races and mountaineering trips.
PHOTO BY JOHN KIRK

CHAPTER 16

TRAINING

YOU MAY FIND your stride and be happy with your current pace and physical abilities. But for some women, the more they do in the backcountry, the more they want to do. It's natural to want to push yourself harder to go farther and faster, and to reach higher and remoter places. If this is you, train for bigger adventures so you can accomplish them.

A full day of training may be hard to pull off during the workweek, but you can squeeze in short, regular routines that get you in shape for weekend outings. Alternate cardiovascular exercise for speed and endurance with weight or resistance training for strength. Training works only if you do it, so pick activities you enjoy, or at least don't hate. Do what works best for you, and be sure to check with your doctor before starting a new exercise regimen.

CARDIO TRAINING

If you have only thirty minutes a day to exercise, use it for cardio. Choose an exercise or combination of exercises like brisk walking, hiking, running outside or on a treadmill, using a stair stepper, cycling, mountain biking, stationary biking, aerobics class, swimming, or doing a cardio workout from a DVD or YouTube channel. You don't have to do all thirty minutes at once. Hop on a stationary bike for ten minutes before breakfast, run on the treadmill at the gym for ten minutes on your lunch hour, and go for a brisk ten-minute walk around your neighborhood after work. The key word here is *brisk*; a leisurely stroll down the street won't cut it.

For the best results, aim to hit and sustain your target heart rate. Your target heart rate is 50 to 85 percent of your maximum "safe" heart rate. Your safe heart rate depends on your age and fitness level, but a general rule of thumb is to subtract your age from 220. This is a guideline; your own maximum and target heart rates could be higher or lower, depending on other factors. If you don't feel well exercising within your target, slow down or stop.

Some exercise equipment can track your heart rate for you. You can also use a wearable heart rate monitor. If you're new to cardio exercise, start slowly with short workouts. Aim to hit the low end of your target heart rate and maintain it as long as you are comfortable. Over time, increase the speed and duration. Once you're getting in thirty minutes of cardio a day within your target range, start alternating between shorter, faster workouts at the high end of your target heart rate and longer, slower ones at the bottom of your target to improve your speed and your endurance.

STRENGTH TRAINING

Training with weights or resistance builds muscle strength and bone density. Once you have a good cardio regimen in place, add thirty minutes of strength training three to five days a week. Just like cardio, you do not have to do all your training at once. You might do ten minutes of ab work at home in the morning and twenty minutes of weightlifting at the gym in the afternoon. Focus primarily on your legs, back, and core, which bear the brunt of your body and pack weight.

Pick a routine that works for your lifestyle. Joining a gym that's near your home or workplace can be a good option. If you can't hold yourself accountable to show up, get an accountability buddy to go with you. If you're new to strength training, hire a trainer to teach you proper form so you don't hurt yourself. If you don't want to join a gym, set up a home gym. You can use free weights, resistance bands, exercise machines, or just a mat and your own body weight to get a good strength-training workout.

Even though you're focusing on your "hiking muscles," it's not a bad idea to hit every muscle group at least once a week for overall strength: back, biceps, pectorals, triceps, deltoids, abdominals, legs, and calves. Once you've identified the exercises you want to do and have learned proper form, do just one set of eight repetitions of each move. Over time, increase to three sets of twelve reps. Then add a little more weight— just 2 to 10 pounds at a time, depending on the weight you start with— with fewer reps and/or sets, and slowly work your way back up to three sets of twelve reps with the new weight. Then add a little more weight and continue the cycle. If you plateau, or stop seeing results with this "pyramiding" style of strength training, try doing drop sets instead, where you do the first, short set with the heaviest weight and lift progressively lighter weights for longer sets to "failure," where you are no longer able to lift the weight. If you don't want to add weight to an exercise, which tends to add mass, you can increase the volume instead by doing more reps per set or more sets per day. Alternating short, dynamic workouts and long, slower ones engages the fast and slow twitch muscles for speed and endurance, respectively, qualities that come in handy when you want to move fast or go the distance.

Cardio and strength training are the two basic components of getting in shape. If you enjoy yoga, Pilates, high-intensity interval training (HIIT, a form of cardio training), training for balance, or any other form of exercise, feel free to include it in your routine. Just don't neglect your cardiovascular health and your strength; you will need both in the backcountry.

If you stop making gains in speed or strength or get bored with your routine, switch it up. Your body adapts to whatever you throw at it, so at some point you should make changes to "wake it up" again. Try different exercises or add something completely new to the mix.

Let your muscles rest between strength-training days. You can either take a complete rest day, or alternate muscle groups to give some muscles a rest while you work others.

Otina Fox works her quads, hamstrings, and calves on a leg-press machine at her local gym. PHOTO COURTESY OF OTINA FOX

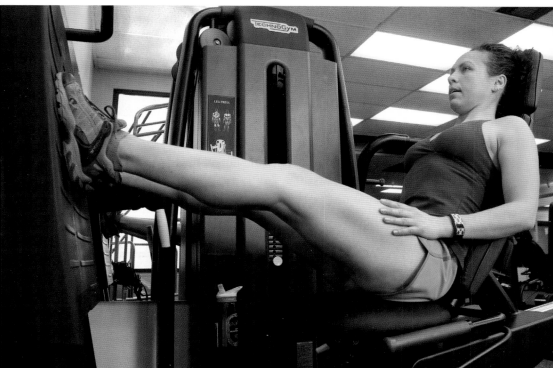

Alyson Kirk is all smiles climbing a steep rockface. Training, rest, and recovery keep her in tip-top shape. PHOTO BY JOHN KIRK

ALYSON KIRK defeated addictions, overcame a life-threatening eating disorder, and survived a high-altitude accident in winter that resulted in a broken femur, persevering to follow her heart in the outdoors. To date, she's finished dozens of 100-mile and 50-mile ultramarathons and 100Ks, winning many of them. In September 2017 she became the second woman and youngest person to finish all 1,313 peaks above 12,000 feet in Colorado. She went on to finish the 11ers and, in 2020, the Colorado 10ers. Her long-term goal is "The Kirk Project": Along with her husband John, she plans to summit every peak above 12,000 feet in the contiguous United States.

Alyson strives to "live life authentically." She says, "When you believe in yourself, despite how the outside world shapes and defines you, you allow remarkable and extraordinary things to happen. Climbing mountains and running ultramarathon races isn't for everyone, and while metaphoric and symbolic in overcoming adversity, so are all the challenges we face to redefine our self-perception. To do remarkable things, we must discover our motivations and develop and cultivate our passions."

REST AND RECOVER

After a big day out, don't feel like you have to rush back into the gym. Get a good night's rest and see how you feel the next day. If you're wiped out, take a rest day. If you're in a lot of pain, see a doctor. If your muscles are sore, either take a rest day or swap your usual routine for a lighter version. Hiking—like any exercise—can cause a buildup of lactic acid in your muscles, making you sore. Gentle stretching, some low-impact cardio, or a light workout can help to break up the lactic acid and lessen the soreness. Another option is a foam roller workout. Applying gentle pressure with the roller acts like a massage and can help work out the kinks. If you use any special equipment at all, follow the instructions or hire a trainer so you don't reinjure yourself.

TRAINING FOR A MAJOR TRIP

If you're planning to do a big trip that's going to push the boundaries of your fitness, ramp up your training to match the demands of the adventure. How early you start training and how hard you train depends on the trip. You may have to carry a heavier pack, hike longer, hike higher, or have more strength. If you have a popular destination in mind—like hiking the Grand Canyon from rim to rim, or climbing Mount Rainier—do some research to find recommended training programs designed specifically for the adventure. Along with physical training, you may have to learn new technical skills, too, so add those to your training schedule. Start researching training plans early; it could take six months or longer to get in good-enough shape and learn the skills you need to tackle a challenge that's beyond your usual activity level.

TAKE STEPS

1. Put together a plan for cardio and strength training. Start small and easy, with ten minutes of each. Do it today and build on it in the coming days.
2. Research nearby gyms and look for places where you can go running so you're not doing all your training at home.
3. If you're out of shape and worried about what you're going to look like at the gym or on the trail, stop it. Whatever you're worried about is a much bigger deal in your head than it is to anyone else. Throw on a T-shirt or tank top, stretchy pants, and sneakers, and go work up a sweat.

Climbers, including the author
(climbing) and (from left to right on
summit) Dennis Jump, Doug Hatfield,
and Darrin Reay rely on teamwork on
an ascent of Independence Monument
in Colorado National Monument.

CHAPTER 17

LEADERSHIP AND TEAM DYNAMICS

IMAGINE BEING ON a group hike. As the day wears on, you struggle to keep up. They're faster than you are, and no matter how hard you push, you get farther and farther behind. Some people stop occasionally to let you catch up, but then they take off again, afraid of being separated from everyone else. Eventually, you're left behind and on your own.

Now imagine being on a backpacking trip and twisting your ankle. You tend to the injury and feel well enough to walk on it, but the pain slows you down. You're carrying a lot of gear, and if you could just lighten your pack by 10 pounds, you'd be able to keep up with everyone. You mention this, hoping the other five people will each offer to take just 2 pounds—a liter of water, perhaps—from your load, but no one even makes eye contact. So you limp on, pushing yourself to stay with the group and wincing with each step.

You wouldn't expect people to treat each other this way, but it happens. Men do it to men. Men do it to women. Women do it to men—and even to other women. *Leadership* and *teamwork* are common terms in the workplace, but they're not always common on the trail, where the stakes are much higher. People's well-being, safety, and even their lives can depend on it.

Formal Leadership

Leadership in the backcountry looks different depending on the group and the adventure. Clubs often assign leaders with certain skills who have completed some sort of training. The extent of these skills may be as basic as knowing how to organize a hike and how to communicate the details with people via e-mail. The training may be basic, too, or it could be extensive and rigorous. When you join a group with an assigned leader—and sometimes co-leader—it's understood that this is the person in charge of making the decisions, or deciding *how* decisions will be made.

Informal Leadership

Informal groups tend to rely on the person who set up the hike or whomever emerges as the natural leader. This could be a person with technical or leadership skills, or someone who simply has a willingness or desire to lead. There isn't always a leader on informal hikes; if you get together with friends to hike, you might just collaborate on navigation, turnaround times, and other decisions, or take turns making decisions and providing guidance depending on individual strengths and skills.

LEADERSHIP STYLES

A person's individual personality plays a large part in their leadership style. You don't have to play a role as a leader, and it's better if you don't. Other people will pick up on the phoniness and you will not gain their trust. It's best to be yourself. If you accept leadership responsibilities, people are trusting you to make decisions that are in their best interest, so you cannot betray that trust. Beyond the responsibilities of a strong leader, which we'll get to shortly, the key to being a good leader is simply respecting the other people on the hike. Strong leaders don't disrespect others. They don't demean or humiliate them. They believe that each person on the team wants to do their best. Good leaders do not see others as slow, lazy, or stupid. They see everyone as unique in their abilities, yet sometimes limited in their technical skills, physical ability, and mental acumen. Leaders appreciate and respect what each person brings to the hike.

Some leaders like to make all the decisions, while others prefer open discussions to get everyone's opinion before making a call. Leaders may also defer to those on the team with specific expertise, depending on the situation. For example, if someone in the group is an expert rock climber and the team needs to cross a technical section, the leader would probably want that person to set up the rope. On a springtime hike in the Rockies, the leader might defer to whomever is most current on their avalanche safety training before deciding whether to climb a snow-packed couloir.

Some leaders are very authoritative. They make the rules and demand that everyone follows them. Though this is seldom an effective outdoor leadership style, there is a time and place for it. In dangerous situations, for example, the leader should be unapologetic about taking charge. If there's a lightning strike close by and the leader orders everyone to turn around and head down, you will be thankful that they yelled instead of quietly taking a poll to see what everyone would like to do. Other times, though, confidence, expertise, and genuine compassion for the group will attract more followers to a leader and inspire a better outcome than harsh words.

If you are unlucky enough to end up with an "alpha male" or "alpha female" hike leader—either formally or informally—who doesn't consider other people's opinions and shuts down people who speak up to offer their knowledge, find someone else to hike with.

LEADERSHIP RESPONSIBILITIES

The leader's responsibilities vary between groups. Your leader may take on all or some of these tasks:

> Organizing the hike, including planning when and where to meet, helping arrange rides between drivers and passengers, and creating a trip plan

> Communicating with the group before the hike, including gathering contact info from everyone and sharing the trip plan and a map

> Providing navigation, orientation, off-trail route-finding, and other skills to complete the trip safely, or assigning an appropriate team member to take on specific tasks that they're qualified to complete

> Setting and maintaining a reasonable pace. Some leaders assign a co-leader or ask someone in the group to hike last to keep track of people who stop for bathroom breaks and clothing adjustments. This way, no one is left behind.

> Assigning temporary leaders on the hike. If there is a large disparity between hiking speeds or if you are hiking through deep snow, the leader may alternate people to the front to take the lead. After, say, five minutes (or fifty paces), the person at the front steps off the trail and then takes their place at the end. Meanwhile, the next person in line takes their place in front.

> Allowing enough stops for rest, snacks, meals, clothing adjustments, photography, and enjoying the views

> Checking in visually and verbally to make sure everyone is okay

> Deciding when to turn around, even if the group hasn't reached their destination

> Keeping the peace between team members

> Risk assessment and emergency situation management

Erica Walter takes up the rear of a team of hikers heading for Crestone Needle in Colorado's Sangre de Cristo Range. PHOTO COURTESY OF OTINA FOX

TEAM RESPONSIBILITIES

People follow an unspoken behavioral protocol in their everyday lives, maintaining a level of civility and manners. You would think these courtesies naturally carry over into the backcountry, but that's not always the case. Competition, self-preservation, and a fear of being seen as weak by others make people behave in strange ways that can create unpleasant and even unsafe situations. It's not a free-for-all out there. If you choose to hike with other people, you choose to be a partner in their experience and their safekeeping. If you don't want that responsibility, hike solo. Otherwise, think of yourself as your sisters' keeper and look out for each other. Self-leadership, common sense, sound judgment, and human compassion will guide you through most situations. Here are a few tips for helping you become a valued team member:

> ❭ Read the trip plan the team leader provides. Pay attention to the meeting time and place, start time and estimated return time,

weather forecast, hiking distance and difficulty, and whether any special gear is recommended or required. If there's a map, download it and bring it with you.

> Share rides to the trailhead with other people in the group to minimize the number of cars on the road. Share expenses, too—if you're not driving, pay for the gas or split the cost with other people in the car.

> At the trailhead, do what you need to do for an on-time start. Take care of clothing adjustments, moving items from your duffel and cooler to your pack, and calibrating or setting options on your GPS, phone app, or other electronic devices. Don't be that one person who holds everyone else up on every hike.

> If you have a particular skill that might be needed, let people know. For example, if you're an EMT, that's good information to share. If someone gets sick or injured, the hike leader will know who to turn to for advice.

> Let the hike leader do their job. Leading a hike can be stressful, especially if the people in the group are disagreeable, whiny, or constantly correcting you.

> Be responsible for your own safety. The hike leader can't see what's going on everywhere all the time.

> Look out for others in your party. If someone has a problem, ask them if they need help. If they say they don't need help, but something is obviously wrong, step in anyway. Someone who's suffering from dehydration may not even know it because they're not thinking clearly. A person who's injured or struggling to keep up may not want to say anything for fear of holding back the group.

> Check in on the leader, too. Leaders often feel like they need to be strong to ensure the safety of the team, but they're human beings, just like you, and they get tired, stressed out, and frustrated. Pay attention to how they are feeling, and don't be afraid to ask how they are and what you could do to make their experience better.

> Backcountry travel isn't a competition. The person who gets to the destination or completes the hike first doesn't win. Being "the fastest and the first" every time will not impress anyone in your group and might even irritate some people.

> Don't split up. Unless you have a good reason for going ahead or being left behind, and you've communicated that to others in your group, stick together.

Great teams make great memories. Linda Parobek, Marsha Hawk, Leigh "Sug" Peterson, and Beth Balser have spent an annual "week in the woods" together for nearly twenty-five years, like this backpacking trip in Wyoming's Snowy Range. PHOTO COURTESY OF BETH BALSER

BETH BALSER, MARSHA HAWK, LINDA PAROBEK, AND LEIGH "SUG" PETERSON, who call themselves the *Colorado Trail 4*, began hiking together to do the Colorado Trail and kept going, exploring Wyoming, Utah, New Mexico, and, currently, Colorado's Wilderness Areas. Beth, Marsha, Linda, and Sug say it's impossible to quantify the lessons learned, laughter shared, and beauty appreciated over the miles, and years. As they grow older, the 12-mile days may be a memory, but they embrace the shorter distances, knowing their time together on the trail is priceless. These women support each other and challenge each other, too. They say, "In all our many adventures, there has never been a cross word. We've overcome fears, rotten weather, being lost, and a ridiculous number of blisters. As a group of women hiking together, we notice and get excited when anyone shows up with a new piece of gear! Where one of us has a weakness, another has a strength. We've created a balance among us that is rich and functional. We eat well, sleep well, and solve the world's problems in camp each evening. Onward we go."

> Don't be afraid to speak up. If you have information the hike leader does not that could affect the outcome of your hike, say something. Don't be a jerk about it, though. If it's not a life-or-death situation, you might want to speak to them one-on-one; if it's an emergency, use your outdoor voice. Even experienced people get into trouble when they rely too heavily on the hike leader or others in the group. Don't be afraid to say, "We are hiking under an avalanche slope," or "This would be a good time to put on our helmets," or "I do not think glissading toward those rocks is a good idea."

BECOMING A LEADER

Not everyone wants to be a leader. Some people have no interest in it, and there's nothing wrong with that. If this is you, then focus on being a good team member instead. If you want to become a leader, take courses and read books on all the technical skills required to lead the kinds of backcountry adventures you'd like to lead, and study leadership, too. Look for outdoor groups in your area that have outdoor leader trainings and certifications, and for leader volunteer opportunities.

TAKE STEPS

1. On your next hike, think about whom in your group is a natural leader and who prefers to follow along. What makes the natural leaders effective and what does not?
2. Check in with people on your next hike. Is anyone struggling to keep up? If you see problems, speak up.
3. Check out leadership training in your area that's specific to outdoor adventure. Even if you don't decide to be a leader, understanding leaders' goals will help you be a better team member.

Goals can motivate you to get out more and go farther, faster, and higher. Here, the author is climbing "The Nipple" on Castle Rock North, Rabbit Valley, Colorado.

CHAPTER 18

SETTING GOALS

OUTDOOR GOALS aren't a requirement, but they can encourage you to get out more often. They can also motivate you to eat better, get regular exercise, and sharpen your technical skills so you can meet them. You can set goals to go farther, faster, or higher—your "personal best," or *PB*. Or you can try to finish a goal faster than anyone else, the "fastest known time," or *FKT*. You can also set your sights on completing a particular "list" of adventures based on topography or designated trails, such as summiting every ranked 14,000-foot peak or hiking every long-distance trail in the contiguous United States. You can even make up your own goals, like increasing your trail mileage every week, and your own lists, like hiking to the top of a local peak every week for a year. If goals interest you, try setting one and see how it goes. If you need help deciding on a particular goal, this chapter will give you some ideas.

DISTANCE, ELEVATION GAIN, AND ALTITUDE PERSONAL BESTS

Figure out how many miles you hiked or how much elevation gain you achieved on your biggest day out, or during a multiday trip. Then plan a trip that takes you farther or adds more elevation gain. Do you know the highest altitude you've ever reached on foot? Is it North Carolina's Mount Mitchell, the highpoint of the Appalachian Mountains? Is it Washington's Mount Rainier, in the Cascade Range? Colorado's Mount Elbert or California's Mount Whitney? Find a higher peak and make a plan to summit it. What's the longest hike you've ever done? Whether it's a 5-mile trail in your favorite forest or the Appalachian Trail, John Muir Trail, Pacific

Crest Trail, or Mountains-to-Sea Trail, there is always another, longer trail to hike. If you've section-hiked a trail (done it one section at a time), try to do more sections at a time, or thru-hike the whole thing. Try to beat your personal bests in distance, elevation, or altitude every year.

FKT (FASTEST KNOWN TIME)

This refers to completing an established goal—a trail, route, or assortment of destinations—faster than any other person's recorded time. It's a speed record. Popular FKT goals include completing long-distance trails and peaks of a certain elevation, such as the Appalachian Trail and Colorado's ranked 14,000-foot summits.

PEAK BAGGING

Peak bagging refers to reaching the summits of every peak on a particular list. There are more peak-bagging lists than you will ever have time to finish in your lifetime, so if you're into elevation and altitude, pick one

Teresa Gergen, the only person to summit every peak over 13,000 feet in the contiguous United States and Hawaii, scrambles across a Class 4 ridge in Wyoming's high country. PHOTO BY ADAM MCFARREN

and go for it. To find premade lists or create your own, read books on mountainous areas you'd like to explore. Check out websites like *Lists of John*, a database of every ranked peak in the continental USA, and source of many, many lists.

HIGHPOINTING

Highpointing refers to gaining the highest point of a particular set of politically or geographically distinct entities. It's not as complicated as it sounds. Country, state, and county highpoints are politically distinct because their borders are not defined by geography. Mountain range and continental highpoints are geographically distinct because they are. You can make a goal of trying to reach the highpoints of continents (the Seven Summits), countries of the world, North American countries, Canadian provinces and territories, American states, contiguous US states, state counties, national forests, wilderness areas, or anything else your heart desires. If your time and resources are limited, having a goal close to home—like highpointing every county in your state—gives you new places to go without breaking the budget. Organizations like the Highpointers Club and the County Highpointers Association provide lots of information to help you get started.

PEAKS BY ELEVATION GOALS

Popular goals such as summiting all the Colorado 14ers—that state's peaks that rise more than 14,000 feet above sea level—and the New Hampshire 4,000 Footers, are based on elevation. These lists have become so popular that during the "peak" summer season, some of the easier summits see more than one thousand summiters in a single day. Websites like *14ers.com* provide information on 14,000-foot summits in Colorado, while sites like *Peakbagger* and *Peakery* list peaks around the world. Once you zero in on a location or goal, get a book on the area to learn more.

PROMINENCE GOALS

Prominence refers to the vertical rise between a summit and the highest saddle between that summit and an adjoining, higher, ranked peak. A *ranked* peak has 300 feet or more of prominence. An *unranked* peak has less than 300 feet of prominence, and a *soft ranked* peak is one whose prominence and status are estimated yet not firmly established as ranked, because the elevation of the summit, the connecting saddle, or both, have not been surveyed, but rather have been determined by interpolation between known contour lines. Note that the 300-foot rule that designates ranking applies in the United States but varies in other countries, especially countries that are home to peaks much higher than 14,000 feet.

Goals based on prominence include summiting every P2K peak, which is a peak with 2,000 or more feet of prominence, and summiting all the ultra-prominence peaks—peaks with 1,500 meters (roughly 5,000 feet) or more—in a state or country. Other lists related to prominence include county summit lists, such as all the ranked peaks in a county.

THE GRID

Doing "the grid" means completing a destination or route—usually summiting a peak—in every month of the year. So "doing the grid" on Pikes Peak means that you hike to the top in every month, though you do not have to do your hikes in consecutive months. A seasonal grid goal requires summiting it just four times—once in each season of calendar spring, summer, fall, and winter. The "calendar" distinction is important: You could be hiking in a whiteout blizzard in March, but if it's the day after the spring equinox, your hike does not count as a winter outing. Sticklers to the rule insist that you must begin and end your hike within the season, so if you're hiking down on the last day of winter and the equinox occurs before you reach the trailhead, it does not count as a true winter hike.

SUMMIT FEVER AND LIST MANIA

Goals are exciting to shoot for and a thrill to achieve. They can take you places you never would have thought to visit and push you beyond what you ever believed possible. Just remember that finishing a goal is secondary to your health and safety. If you get into a dicey situation, turn around—even if it's your final peak on a list or final mile on a long-distance trail. You can always come back another day when there's no lightning, or avalanche danger, or forest fire. Enjoy your lists and your goals, and live to hike again.

TAKE STEPS

1. Think about what you like to do and what you would like to do more of: hike higher, longer, or faster. Write down some goals that could help you accomplish that.
2. Visit peak bagging, highpointing, and other websites to get an idea of the many lists available. Decide whether any of them appeal to you, and whether you are capable of completing them.
3. Once you've chosen a goal, head to your local library or outdoor retailer to find books and maps on the subject and plan a trip to get started.

Trip planning increases your odds of success, especially on complicated treks, climbs, and alpine adventures. On a high peak in Wyoming, Teresa Gergen and Jim Rickard discuss their location and route.
PHOTO BY ADAM MCFARREN

CHAPTER 19

TRIP PLANNING

FOLLOWING OTHER people's trip plans is a convenient introduction to new places and trails, but at some point, learn how to plan your own trips. Step through the questions below, create a trip plan, and test it on an outing. Use it as a template and revise it for every new trip.

WHY

Think about why you want to do the trip. You may just have a day off and want to get outside. Or you could be working on a goal and this trip is an opportunity to improve your personal best or complete something on a list. Your reason can be as simple as "I've never planned a trip before and I'd like to give it a try."

WHERE

Where do you want to go? Maybe there's a national forest, park, or a wilderness area you like, or one you've never explored. Or you might have a more specific destination in mind like a lake, waterfall, or summit. Start small and local and expand your trips as you improve your planning skills.

WHEN

Look at your calendar and pick a day or more that you have open. You'll need time to get to the trailhead, do your adventure, and drive home. If you can't find that kind of time, then adjust your "where" to someplace closer for now.

WHAT

Think about what you want to accomplish. Maybe you're using this trip to practice your map and compass skills, your GPS skills, or how to use a new phone app. Or you have a new tent, stove, or sleeping system you want to test. You could be doing your first snowshoe or trying out crampons for the first time. Consider your time frame, physical fitness, and skills. You don't want to get in over your head, but it's okay to push yourself, too. You can always turn around.

WHO

As your vision comes together, think about people who might like to come along. Talk to them about it and gauge their interest. See if your proposed dates line up with their availability.

HOW

You've done some research on the area you want to visit, but now you have to dig deeper. Visit the website of the land area. Look for information

If you plan to visit a place often, invest in a map of the area.

specific to your route or trail. Download a map, buy one, or make one. If it's an area you expect to visit many more times, check your local library, bookstore, or gear shop and get a guidebook.

Pay special attention to dates and times the area is open to the public, fees, and if you plan to camp, whether they allow it. If they do, note whether reservations are required. Look for information like limits on group sizes, fire restrictions, whether pets are allowed (if you are bringing a dog), and updates like fire restrictions and trail closures. If there's a ranger district assigned to the region, call them for the latest information on trail conditions. Also, check your state's department of transportation site for road conditions and closures.

Popular areas in the United States tend to have entire websites and online discussion forums dedicated to them. A website where people report on their experiences and answer questions can be a great resource.

Start documenting your plan and make adjustments as you get more information. E-mail it to the other people on your trip so they have time to study it and prepare.

WHICH BACKCOUNTRY ADVENTURE IS BEST FOR ME?

When you're trying to decide which hikes to choose, keep these factors in mind:

› **Your time frame.** How much time you have will dictate what's feasible and what doesn't make sense. Rushing to finish a hike and get home by a certain time is stressful and can be dangerous. Estimate the time it would take to do the hike by yourself and add extra time for each person who comes along.

› **Your fitness, speed, and skill.** Don't get in over your head with a hike that's too long, too difficult, or too complicated for your abilities.

› **Hike distance (mileage).** Make sure you'll be able to go the distance within your available time.

› **Elevation gain.** How many feet you gain in elevation can add a lot of time and difficulty to your hike.

› **Destination.** Heading to a special place gives you something to look forward to on your hike.

Trips in guidebooks are almost always on legally accessible, public lands.

› **Sights along the way.** Not all hikes lead to a destination, but most are in scenic areas with views of creeks, mountain ridges, meadows, and overlooks along their routes that add to their attractiveness.

› **Terrain.** Details about a hike's terrain aren't always easy to find, but some guidebooks and trail descriptions provide this information. Mixed terrain takes longer to navigate than an established trail.

› **Driving distance.** Use an online map site search or phone app to determine the distance and driving time to the trailhead.

› **Roads to the trailhead.** Make sure the route to the trailhead is passable in your vehicle at the time of year you're going. Some roads are inaccessible by passenger car or closed to all vehicles during the winter.

› **Private property.** Guidebooks typically don't list hikes that are on private property, but hikes you find on the internet or hear about through word of mouth may not be legally accessible. Stick to public lands and avoid getting into trouble with a landowner.

YOUR TRIP PLAN

A trip plan can be simple or complicated, depending on the trip. Following is a list of what you might want to include in yours.

› **Trip name:** Give it a meaningful name. Instead of calling it "Trip A" or "Keisha's Hike," call it "Pikes Peak from the Crags," for example.

› **Contacts:** The names and phone numbers of everyone who's going, an emergency contact who knows where you are going and the route you're taking, and the number of the local ranger district or other land entity.

› **Short description of the trip:** Where you're going and the destination(s) you expect to reach or highlights of the route.

› **Departure date, time, and meeting place, estimated return date and time, plus carpooling recommendations:** Choose a meeting spot where people can leave their vehicles, like a public parking lot. Request that people carpool and see who wants to drive and who wants to ride. Get the details sorted out *before* the day of the trip.

› **Name of the trailhead and directions:** If you're heading to a campground first, include the name and directions to that, too.

› **Recommended gear:** People should know the basics, but if special gear is required, such as WAG bags or bear canisters, note that in the plan. Depending on how experienced your group is, you can add more details, such as how much food and fuel to bring.

› **Shared gear plans:** If five people are joining you, you don't need six tents and six stoves. Work that out ahead of time.

› **Weather forecast:** The current forecast for your trip date(s), including the temperature range and chances of precipitation and a link to the NOAA website or other weather site so people can check for changing weather predictions.

› **Map and route description:** Include trail names, distance, elevation gain, and terrain. If you're planning a backpack, include information on where you expect to set up camp each night. If your partners like to buy their own maps, recommend one that covers the area.

› **Sunrise and sunset times, and turnaround time:** Turning around can be a sore point for people set on making their destination come hell or high water. You might want to add a note explaining your reason behind the turnaround time, such as "We will be turning around at noon to avoid hiking out in the dark . . . to avoid softening snow and fallen snow bridges and increased avalanche danger . . . to get back to the trailhead and camp early enough to make dinner while it's still light out . . . to avoid driving home in rush-hour traffic."

› **Permits or fees:** What they are, how much they cost, and who's responsible for them.

Once you've finalized your plan and shared it with your trip partners, share it with someone who is *not* going on the trip. Also tell them the latest time you will call to say you're safe and back at the trailhead or campsite. This isn't always necessary, and may not be possible if you're in a remote area, but if you are hiking on demanding terrain, in uncertain weather, or anywhere that carries a high risk, do it. Make sure they have your phone number and a description of your car—make, model, color, year, and license plate number—so if you don't call, they can pass that information on to emergency personnel. Recommend to others in your party that they do the same. And don't forget to follow up—call your "emergency contact" from the trailhead so they can relax.

TAKE STEPS

1. Step through the why, what, etc. portions of this chapter to figure out where you want to go. Figure out whether your trip makes sense based on your time frame and skills.

2. Create a trip plan. Try it out, see how it goes, and update it when you get home with everything you wish you had included in it.

3. Standardize a trip plan template. This way, whenever you start planning a trip, or are even thinking about planning one, you can plug in details that you learn in your research.

Alyson Kirk maintains a high success rate on reaching her goals with training and the right attitude.
PHOTO BY JOHN KIRK

CHAPTER 20

STRATEGIES FOR SUCCESS

A WOMAN IN THE WILD can do everything right and still fall short of her vision for success. Success, by the way, means whatever you want it to mean. It's your vision—not someone else's. When you start comparing yourself and your accomplishments to other people and what they're doing, you're destined to fail right from the start. Other people do things for *their* reasons. You do *you*—for *your* reasons. Hiking, camping, and backcountry travel isn't a competition; it's a way of life. If your adventures don't make you happy, think about why. The only rules for success are those you impose on yourself.

BE RESPONSIBLE FOR YOURSELF

Conventional wisdom dictates that there is safety in numbers, and you can benefit from the wisdom of the crowd in the backcountry. However, relying solely on the opinions and judgment of others can also put you at risk. The most vocal person in your group isn't always the most knowledgeable or prudent, and they may define success differently than you. That person might think getting to the top of a mountain is the first priority, even if there's a lightning storm brewing. You, on the other hand, think it's more important to get back to the trailhead alive. There's a tendency to feel more confident in a crowd, and the more experienced the group, the less likely anyone is to question others' decisions. This can lead to errors in judgment that put everyone's well-being at risk. The bottom line is that your safety is your responsibility. Take it upon yourself to continue

Otina Fox takes in the view at Iceberg Lakes in Glacier National Park, Montana. A successful hike is whatever you envision it to be. PHOTO COURTESY OF OTINA FOX

your backcountry education, prepare properly for trips, and speak up if you disagree with someone else's decisions.

REALISTIC GOAL SETTING

If you're not satisfied with your progress, you could be reaching a little too high too soon. Be realistic about your expectations. Are you physically capable of doing what you want to do? If your goal is to do something that you will probably never be physically capable of, allow yourself to pick another goal.

Consider your motivation. Do you actually *want* to do what you set out to do, or do you simply want to have done it? There's a big difference. You may want to hike the Grand Canyon from Rim to Rim to Rim because your best friend did it. But if you despise long, hot hikes, then why do it? Likewise, if you're thinking of climbing Mount Rainier to impress your friends but you hate hiking in the cold—or crevasses terrify you—skip it. Choose a goal that you *want* to do—that you look forward to doing.

Not every moment of every adventure is lollipops and rainbows. Most real challenges come with a certain amount of suffering. But if you are dreading a trip, don't do the trip. You can change your goals anytime you like. Take them down a notch, give yourself more time to complete them, or change them completely. Life and work are hard enough without coming up with new ways to torture yourself when you're supposed to be having fun.

PHYSICAL TRAINING

If you feel like the goals you set for yourself are achievable but you're still struggling to meet them, you may need more training. If you're already doing cardio and strength training, bump it up a notch. Train harder or devote more time to it. Fine-tune it to fit your goals. Your training regimen may not be right for you—everyone's physiology is different. Try something new. Check out classes at your gym and sign up for Pilates, Spin, Zumba, CrossFit, kickboxing, or yoga. For cardio, swap trail running for mountain biking. For strength training, swap free weights for resistance bands. If you're sick of the treadmill, try the stair stepper, and if all your workouts are indoors, get outside. Training boredom and burnout don't provide the motivation you need to keep pushing hard so you're ready for your next adventure. If you need more motivation, get a training buddy or hire a coach.

SKILLS TRAINING

Skills develop over time. If you aren't competent enough to orient yourself in the backcountry, or set up a tent and make a meal, or administer basic first aid, get some skills training. Read books that dive more into these topics, get your hiking buddies to study with you, and practice. Find a mentor, attend workshops, or take courses from a professional school. Don't ever feel bad about not knowing how to do something. Anything you don't know yet, you can learn. Backcountry skills aren't taught in traditional school, and we don't use most of them at work. This is new territory, so give yourself a break. Then make a plan to fill in your technical gaps with learning and practice.

THE MENTAL GAME

You may know when you don't have the physical abilities or technical skills to accomplish a goal, but those are only part of what determines your success. The bigger piece is what goes on inside your head: the mental game. Outdoor adventure taxes your brain. It demands all your attention. You are going places you've never been, doing things you've never done. Sometimes you have to press on past the point of fun. Sometimes, when it's hard and relentless, it comes down to how much you're willing to suffer. All of this messes with your head. More than anything else you bring to an adventure, your mental strength and endurance will get you through the toughest times.

One method for dealing with the demands of the trail is to focus on short-term objectives. If you're on a 12-mile hike, don't think "Twelve miles—*ack!*" Think "Three miles to the trail junction." Then, "Three miles to the top of the pass." "Three miles to the river . . . the lake . . . camp!" Take regular breaks to snack, rest, drink, and study the map. When you start doing longer hikes, count your steps to see how many paces—a step with a left foot and a right foot—it takes to cover one-tenth of a mile. Then, when you're hiking back to camp after a long day, you can count your steps to keep your mind busy. If you have a mile to go and you cover a tenth of a mile in 100 paces, then count 100 paces ten times and you'll be at camp. This isn't a very exciting technique, but it takes your mind off the mileage, and it's especially helpful when you're hiking out in the dark and you don't have anything to look at except the circle of light from your headlamp.

The best way to beef up your mental game is to practice. The more difficulties you endure, the better you'll be able to handle them again. Sometimes just knowing that you've endured something hard gives you enough belief in yourself to keep going. Remembering how it feels to be done, too, can be massively inspiring. "This sucks," you think to yourself. "My feet hurt, my back aches, I'm really hungry, and I have to pee. But as long as I keep going it will eventually end." And then there will be coffee and doughnuts and pizza and beer. Maybe tacos. *Mmm . . . tacos.*

That might sound pretty silly, but focusing on the pleasures at the end of the trail or at camp—taking off your boots, dropping your pack, getting some food in your belly, and stretching out on a sleeping pad under the stars—will help you press on.

Of course, don't neglect your health just to keep going. If you have a blister, stop to take care of it. If you haven't eaten for hours, have a snack.

Find a log, sit down, take off your pack, and look around at where you are. Appreciate the moment and consider how wonderful it is to be in it.

Finally, talk to your hiking buddies. On a long hike, a good conversation can make time on the trail fly by. On a challenging hike, it can calm your nerves. This is where you will really appreciate your chatty hiking partner who can talk for hours. Bonus points if she's had a lot of adventures and knows how to tell a good story.

These are just some ideas, and you will discover your own methods for pushing your mind and body farther than you have before. Set the bar as low or as high as you like. Define your success, then go get it.

TAKE STEPS

1. Evaluate your physical training and decide whether it's time for a change.
2. Evaluate your technical skills. If you're struggling with something, take a course, read a book, watch a video, and ask a friend to train for that particular skill with you.
3. Think about the trips you've done. Which ones did you enjoy the most, and why? Plan more of those types of adventures, in those kinds of areas, on that type of terrain, with those kinds of people. Push yourself to try new things, but never abandon what you love most.

More adventure awaits beyond the beaten path. Here, the author scrambles down from the Mount Russell summit in California's Sierra Nevada Mountains.
PHOTO BY DOUGLAS HATFIELD

NEXT STEPS

Jean Aschenbrenner approaches
the summit of Mount Wilson
in Colorado's San Miguel
Mountains on a cold, breezy
morning in January.
PHOTO BY KEN NOLAN

CHAPTER 21

HIGH-ALTITUDE MOUNTAINEERING

AMONG LIFE'S EXPERIENCES, few come close to standing on a mountaintop. Pushing yourself to a high place above the clouds brings a sense of accomplishment, and the payoff—the view—is hard to match on any other adventure.

Yet, thousands of feet above sea level, the environment challenges you with new demands. The reduced barometric pressure and decrease in oxygen taxes your body, making you susceptible to dehydration and altitude-induced illnesses. Weather is more extreme, the terrain more varied and less forgiving. Then there's gravity: the higher you go, the farther you could fall.

This chapter is an introduction to high-altitude mountaineering and does not attempt to provide a thorough understanding of all the expertise and training required to safely pursue the sport. It is applicable for high-altitude hikes in the contiguous United States, and to about 20,000 feet in some countries. If you plan to climb higher, or in colder regions such as Canada and Alaska, seek out other sources for health, nutrition, clothing, gear, weather, and terrain advice. If you're new to mountaineering, find a mentor, hire a guide, or join a group with an experienced leader to take you on your first high-altitude trips. A word of caution: Mountaineering can be addictive. Once you get your first peak, you may never settle for sea-level adventures again.

ALTITUDE AND YOUR HEALTH

Though high altitude usually refers to elevations of 8,000 feet or more above sea level, some people are affected as low as 6,000 feet. How much altitude affects you depends on how well your body naturally acclimatizes; preexisting conditions that make you susceptible to altitude-induced sicknesses; and the time and effort you put into acclimatization.

Some people barely feel the effects of altitude at all, while others are more severely affected.

Hyperventilation and Asthma

Hiking at high elevations can bring on hyperventilation and asthma attacks in some people. If you are prone to either condition, pay attention to early symptoms and treat them immediately. Hyperventilation can be calmed by intentionally slowing your breathing, pinching off one nostril at a time and alternating breaths, breathing into your belly instead of your chest, and by breathing into a paper bag. If someone on your trip is hyperventilating and cannot control it on their own, make eye contact with them, breathe slowly and deeply, and encourage them to match your breaths. If you suffer from asthma, treat it as you normally would. With either affliction, if the condition doesn't improve, descend.

Acute Mountain Sickness

Acute mountain sickness (AMS) is a mild form of altitude sickness. Symptoms include headaches, dizziness, shortness of breath, and nausea. People typically acclimatize within a few days at altitude, but if you suffer from AMS, either descend or remain at the current elevation until the symptoms subside. Have a snack and a drink and treat headaches with ibuprofen. You might think you can keep going up, powering through a headache and nausea, but if your health deteriorates, you may not be able to get yourself down.

High-Altitude Pulmonary Edema (HAPE) and High-Altitude Cerebral Edema (HACE)

HAPE and HACE are more serious conditions that can lead to death. With HAPE, fluid from blood vessels leaks into the air sacs of the lungs, making it difficult to breathe. Symptoms include shortness of breath while resting, a persistent cough, tightness in the chest, breathing that produces a crackling or wheezing sound, coughing up frothy or bloody sputum, and rapid breathing or heart rate. A person with HAPE may even start to turn blue, especially around the mouth, due to a lack of oxygen.

With HACE, fluid leaks into the brain tissue, causing it to swell. Symptoms of HACE include disorientation, fatigue, fever, eye sensitivity to light, and eventually visible swelling of the face and head. HAPE and HACE should be treated by descending and seeking immediate medical attention.

Preventing Altitude Sicknesses

Prepare for hiking at altitude by doing increasingly higher hikes, adding 1,000 feet on subsequent outings. See how your body reacts, and don't go higher until you feel well enough. If you're traveling to a place located at a higher elevation with the goal of hiking even higher, add a day or more to the front of the trip and use that time to acclimatize. Hike around town the first day, then do increasingly higher hikes each day if you can. Take it easy, though; don't push yourself, or you'll wear out your legs for your "big day." Acclimatization at your destination isn't always possible when you're traveling on a limited timetable. If you live in an area where you can hike to higher elevations, make that part of your training before your trip.

NUTRITION AND HYDRATION AT ALTITUDE

Due to the extra demands on your body at altitude, it is especially important to pay attention to your food and drink intake. Make regular stops to snack and drink—even if you don't feel like it. Carry nutritionally dense, high-calorie foods that taste good and deliver long-lasting energy. Depending on your metabolism and your route, you could burn 200 to 1,000 calories an hour on a high-altitude hike, so listen to your body and give it what it needs. Up your fluid intake, too. Start hydrating in the days leading up to the trip. On the mountain, try to ingest about 50 percent more water and electrolyte drinks per hour than you would on a typical low-elevation hike and see how you feel. You may have to take more pee breaks, but it will be worth it to ensure the benefits of staying hydrated.

HIGH-ALTITUDE CLOTHING AND GEAR

Your regular hiking clothes work for high altitude, too, but you may need more layers to protect you from the more extreme, changing weather conditions and temperature swings. Sturdy, mid-rise mountaineering boots protect your feet and provide traction on the rougher terrain. Consider a heavier-weight mountaineering sock, an added sock liner, or even a second pair of socks. You may need more insulating layers for warmth and sturdier hardshell layers to protect you from the wind. Mountaineering gloves and shell mitts, which are thin, windproof mittens, may also be required, depending on the temperature and wind speed. Carry a hooded rain jacket anytime you hike up high. If you get wet at elevation, it could take a while to hike below tree line or to shelter.

For hiking on snow at altitude, swap your sunglasses for *glacier glasses*, which provide a better seal around your eyes and prevent light seepage. Glacier glasses have flexible temples for a snug fit and a retainer to keep them from flying off in high winds. On extremely windy days, wear *goggles* instead. These provide an even more secure fit and protect your eye area from sun, wind, and snow. Some glacier glasses and goggles have vents to reduce fogging. If you have fogging problems, wipe the lenses with a soft microfiber cloth, or use Cat Crap or other anti-fog lens cleaner. In a pinch, use a little spit.

Depending on the conditions and the difficulty of your high-altitude adventure, you may need additional gear, such as an ice axe, rock climbing gear, ice climbing gear, skis, or snowshoes. Research the route, get proper training so you know how to use the gear, and pack accordingly.

At high altitude, make sure everything is attached to you, your pack, or, if you're wearing one, your harness. Loop glove leashes around your wrists so that if you remove a glove it isn't swept away in the wind. Likewise, attach your water bottle to your pack with a cordelette or a loop of nylon cord so that if it slips through your hands it doesn't careen down the mountainside. The same goes for snowshoes, ice axes, and all other gear. Don't underestimate the power of the wind at higher elevations; you should expect it to carry everything away that isn't tied down. Similarly, if you drop a piece of clothing or gear high on a mountainside, it could slide or fall thousands of feet and you will never recover it.

CAMPING AND COOKING AT HIGH ALTITUDE

Up high, exposed to extreme temperatures and high winds, your tent takes a beating. If possible, camp below tree line to take advantage of the natural protection. Though tree line varies across the United States depending on geography, climate, and exposure, American alpine timberline is typically around 12,000 feet. Depending on where you set up camp, you might need a sturdier mountaineering tent instead of a standard camping tent. Set up your tent in a protected area out of the wind. Stay away from deposition zones below slopes where rockfalls or avalanches might slide into your camp. This can be tricky because the leeward side, away from the wind and often on the eastern aspect of a mountain, is also the side most likely to slide, whereas the windblown, windward aspect is less snow-packed but also more exposed to the wind. When you set up your tent, pay attention to wind direction so you don't get blasted every time you step out the door. Anchor the tent firmly to the ground and use the guy lines for more security. If there is snow available, use it to build a protective wall against the wind near your tent.

A tent with a vestibule that you can cook in is preferable. Don't ever cook in a closed tent or a vestibule that isn't made for cooking; without proper ventilation, a stove's fumes can cause death by asphyxiation. Keep in mind that your isobutane canister stove may not perform well or even work at all at high altitude. Buy or borrow a liquid fuel stove and practice lighting it before a trip.

The saying "train high, sleep low" is a good rule to follow. Training at altitude helps you acclimatize while sleeping closer to sea level lets you recover. However, sometimes sleeping high can't be avoided. If you've never done it, prepare for a rough night. Camping at altitude, less oxygen and the resulting hypoxia can hinder your breathing and affect sleep. It's common to feel wide awake in the tent, even when you're exhausted and want to sleep. Traditional sleep aids can interfere with breathing, so they are not a viable option. They *could* cause you to stop breathing. The good news is that if you have a multiday trip, the first night may be the worst; your body should adjust over time so that consecutive nights are more restful. If you do feel like you're awake all night, stay put. Resting your body is important even if your mind is awake, and you will probably drift in and out of sleep.

To improve your chances of a decent night's sleep, avoid eating for an hour before bed. Don't go to bed hungry, either, which could also affect your sleep. Avoid foods and drinks that contain sugar, caffeine, or alcohol—all can keep you up. It's tempting to have a late snack and a nip before hitting the tent, but plan ahead and eat early, then spend the last hour of the day relaxing with a quiet conversation or a good book. Make a point to go to the bathroom so you're less likely to wake up in the middle of the night. Keep a liter of water in the tent so if you wake up thirsty you can get a quick sip without getting up, and have your FUD nearby so that if you do have to pee, you're not fumbling for it in the dark. If you're in a noisy area and other people want to stay up late, just excuse yourself, put in some earplugs, and go to bed. You will feel much better in the morning.

TERRAIN AND LAND NAVIGATION AT ALTITUDE

Land navigation at high altitude can be easier because you are out of the trees and have more visibility of the land around you. The topography is more obvious. The terrain does tend to be less forgiving, though, so you

Terrain at high altitude can be more varied and demanding. PHOTO COURTESY OF OTINA FOX

have to be more thoughtful of your route. If you're following a trail at elevation, be aware of unstable terrain on and above your path. Loose rocks can pop out under your feet or tumble down on you. A path that was safe one year may have eroded away in monsoon flooding or could be buried in deadfall caused by seasonal avalanching. When you're navigating in the mountains, forego the quickest route for the safest one. This might involve contouring across a slope in a switchback pattern to reach a summit instead of going straight up. It might mean aiming for a saddle instead of the highpoint so you can approach the summit from a lower angle. Don't choose a route that's so long it could put you in danger of being on a mountain later than you're prepared for—in other words, don't get stuck in a lightning storm or have to do an unplanned bivouac. Weigh the advantages and the risks between your options and choose a route that's safe, within your abilities, and allows you to do the peak in the time you have available.

Mountain topography can slow you down considerably. Account for that in your trip planning. It takes longer to hike uphill than to cross a plain. You are more likely to run across scree, talus, and boulder fields, rock gullies, and snow couloirs. Mixed terrain takes more time and requires more vigilance than consistent, level ground, taking a toll both physically and mentally.

High-altitude terrain also tends to be fragile. Though tundra in some areas of the world is protected by permafrost, land above tree line in the Lower 48 drains continuously and is susceptible to damage caused by human foot traffic. High-altitude plant life has a short growing season, so regrowth of damaged areas takes many years. Treading on plant life damages the plant and affects the animals that depend on it for nourishment. Take all of this into consideration when you plan your route and avoid delicate areas.

WEATHER AT ALTITUDE

Extreme weather is common at higher elevations and retreating to safety isn't always easy, or fast. You can't just hide in the trees when you're above tree line. You can't scramble down wet ledges as quickly as you climbed them when they were dry. Due to the elevation, distance, and terrain involved in gaining altitude, descending takes time even in good weather. In bad weather, you might feel panicked, making the situation worse.

Avoid getting into bad weather at high altitude. Pay attention to the forecast and monitor it regularly during your outing. Research the area and familiarize yourself with trends. Some areas see lightning storms or monsoon rains with regularity during certain months. If you're visiting a new area, find people who adventure there regularly and pick their brains about what to expect. You can also get guidebooks to the area and read the section on weather, or call the land management office to get the latest insight into weather trends.

ALTITUDE TRAINING

Like all outdoor adventure training, preparing for high altitude includes cardiovascular and strength training. Since the environment is even more unpredictable and extreme and a descent takes more time, being physically fit, strong, and fast is a matter of safety.

If you're planning your first high-altitude trip, ramp up your training. Consider how much weight you'll be carrying and make sure your legs and back are strong enough and that you can move fast enough to meet your schedule. Add uphill hikes, preferably on similar terrain, to your training plan. If there are no peaks nearby, use a stair-stepper machine at your gym to develop your quadriceps, hamstrings, and calves. Bring your pack to the gym, stuff a towel in the bottom, and add plates to simulate the weight of your gear. Start light—you don't want so much weight in your pack that you fall off the stepper. Then add one small plate at a time.

Train for the higher altitude by gradually increasing your elevation on consecutive trips. If you're heading out of state or out of the country to climb higher than you're used to, spend the weeks leading up to the trip hiking as high as you can on your local mountains so you'll be acclimatized. Then take a few days—or even a week—off to rest your legs for the big trip.

Jean Aschenbrenner descends the southwest couloir below Mount Wilson's summit. Though she needs both hands free for the scramble, her ice axe is securely tethered to her pack so she can access it quickly and without fear of dropping it. PHOTO BY KEN NOLAN

ACCIDENTS AT HIGH ALTITUDE

When you're injured on a mountain and you can't get out on your own, you may need to call for help. The odds are improved if you have a SPOT (Synchronized Pre-Deployment and Operational Tracker), PLB, or cell-phone coverage and can get your location out, and if you're on a known route that search-and-rescue personnel can follow. If you're stranded on the side of a mountain in unfamiliar, potentially dangerous terrain, an

JEAN ASCHENBRENNER is a retired engineer who has always loved adventuring in the outdoors. In 1993 she was the first woman (and fourth person) to summit all 637 of the peaks over 13,000 feet in Colorado. Jean's serious outdoor adventuring began at age twenty-two with a four-day backpack in the mountains above Aspen. She had a World War II backpack from a flea market, a Green Stamps sleeping bag, Pop-Tarts, raisins, and a chunk of cheese. She met wonderful people and has been going strong ever since. Jean likes both solo trips and going with good friends. She has backpacked, backcountry skied, rock climbed, ice climbed, canoed, canyoneered, climbed many of Colorado's peaks in winter, and climbed peaks over 22,000 feet. These days, you can find Jean backpacking in New Zealand or Italy's Dolomites, hiking from hut to hut. Jean says, "As you get older, just keep going. Find easier trails, lighten your pack, but keep going!"

evacuation could take hours, or even days. Prevention is the best way to avoid an accident. Before venturing to higher elevations—especially off-trail—make sure someone knows where you're going, your planned route, and when you'll be back. Double-check your pack to make sure you have all the clothing, gear, food, water, and first-aid items you need to prevent a bad situation. Know the route, and bring whatever you need to navigate safely and avoid venturing into risky territory.

Some women carry overnight gear like a sleeping bag and a tent or bivy sack in case they're injured or lost and stranded. While the extra weight may slow you down, it could also save your life. Consider the advantages and the risks of carrying more or less gear. If you or someone in your party is injured and you can't get out on your own, call for help (if you're able) and give your location and details of the injured party to the emergency professionals. Use your first-aid skills to do what you can to provide relief to the patient and prevent additional injury. Then try to find a protected area out of the elements to wait it out. If the person has a back injury, you may not be able to move them. Keep yourself and the injured person warm and dry, using clothing or gear to insulate yourselves from the cold ground and ward off chilling winds. Eat and drink to keep your strength and your spirits up until help arrives.

High-altitude mountaineering offers new challenges, but it's within your abilities. On many routes, it's simply a longer hike to a higher place with better views. You may never have to deal with the dangers, but be aware of them and plan accordingly to mountaineer safely.

TAKE STEPS

1. Think about the challenges at altitude and how you might need to change up your clothing and gear to meet them. Make a list of what you may need to buy before doing a high-altitude trip.
2. Start training for high altitude. Train harder, higher, and with more pack weight. If you need to work on your technical skills, take a formal course and practice.
3. Look at where you've been and determine the highest altitude you've reached. Plan a trip that takes you a little higher and see how your body responds. If you do well at altitude, consider a bigger trip three months, six months, or even a year out to a much higher place and start training for it. Find some hiking buddies willing to train with you.

The author keeps her eyes and skin protected from the sun, cold, and wind on a long winter hike.
PHOTO BY DOUG HATFIELD

CHAPTER 22

WINTER IN THE WILDERNESS

WINTER BRINGS colder temperatures and in some parts of the country, snow. Winter outings afford new challenges to a woman in the wild, but exciting experiences, too. With the right clothing, gear, skills, and attitude, winter could become your favorite season. Though calendar winter lasts only from mid-December to mid-March, wintry conditions can exist from fall through spring, and at higher altitudes, freezing temperatures and blizzards can occur any time of year. Even if you plan to hike only from springtime through the fall, understanding the demands of winter-like travel come in handy year-round.

WINTER WEATHER

The consequences of being unprepared in winter weather can be dire, so review weather forecasts leading up to the day of your hike and be aware of changing conditions on the trail. Pay close attention to the predicted temperature range, the wind speed and direction, and the wind chill factor. All are listed on the National Weather Service's site. Also check the visibility, which could affect your ability to navigate, and the expected chances of precipitation and total accumulation.

Precipitation in the form of freezing rain, sleet, hail, graupel, and snow is common in some parts of the country, especially at high elevations. Though they all come from the same source, each has a different structure. Freezing rain falls as a liquid. Instead of bouncing off clothing, freezing rain clings to it. When you're out of the weather and in the protection of your tent, freezing rain melts, soaking your clothing and bedding. If you get stuck in freezing rain, keep out the cold with insulating layers and cover up with a waterproof protective layer too.

Sleet (basically, frozen rain) and graupel (ice-covered snow) both tend to bounce off outerwear, so stopping to put on waterproof clothing isn't always necessary. If you do start to get wet, however, put on a rain jacket. Hail falls as chunks of ice, and, depending on the size, can be very painful if it hits you. In a hailstorm, you might need a snug-fitting cap, a puffy hooded jacket, and a hooded raincoat to keep you dry and protect your head from injury. Snow varies in consistency from dry, fluffy champagne powder to wet, heavy slush. All precipitation can create slick trails.

Warm gloves, winter gaiters, facemasks, chemical warmers, glacier glasses, and goggles keep you warm, dry, and protected from sun and wind in winter months.

The hike may start off in sunshine and blue skies, but winter weather can come in fast and hard, creating a dangerous situation. Don't underestimate it—be prepared for the worst.

STAYING HEALTHY IN WINTER

Cold, wind, and snow make for an invigorating hike if you're prepared for them. They also put you at risk for hypothermia, windburn, frostnip, frostbite, and snow blindness. Prepare for the cold and wind by following the precautions in chapter 9, "Staying Healthy," and treating cold- and wind-caused injuries and illness per guidelines found in chapter 10, "First Aid."

Snow blindness is caused by too much UV light hitting your eyes—basically a sunburn on your corneas, the thin outer layers of your eyeballs. In winter, the sun beats down on you and sunlight reflects off the snow, so wearing either glacier glasses or goggles that protect the sides as well as the front of your eyes is critical to keep out UV rays. If you don't own either, at least wear sunglasses with a 400 UV rating and put glacier glasses on your list. For high winds, go with goggles. Snow blindness is painful and debilitating. If you're blinded in the backcountry, you'll have to depend on others to get you out. Snow blindness usually heals on its own after a few days, but it can be permanent.

Some people are more sensitive to the cold than others. People with Raynaud's disease, where blood vessels react to the cold by narrowing,

limiting blood flow, should be extra careful venturing out. The best prevention is to dress in more, warmer layers; avoid skin exposure by wearing
gloves, a snug-fitting knitted or fleece cap, a buff, glasses or goggles, and
a facemask if necessary; stay dry and out of the wind; and remember to
eat and drink.

WINTER NUTRITION AND HYDRATION

Winter trips burn more calories. It takes more energy to travel in the cold,
especially when you're trudging through snow and carrying a heavier pack
full of winter gear. The cold doesn't increase your appetite, though, so you're
more likely to be calorie-deficient. Make a point to eat at regular intervals.

Pack foods that don't freeze or get so hard you can't eat them. Some
trail bars fare better in cold temps than others, so try a few to see which
ones work for you. Food that would typically go bad on a warm day is safe
to carry in winter, so feel free to make sandwiches and wraps with all the
veggies and condiments. If it's refrigerator-cold out, they won't go bad.

Pack hot drinks, too: soup, tea, hot cocoa, and vegetable bouillon
make a great addition to your trailside lunch. Avoid alcohol, which con-
stricts blood vessels and makes you colder. Before you leave the house
for a winter hike, boil some water and add a powdered drink mix in your
water bottle, then tuck it into an insulated parka. You'll have a hot, sweet
drink to kick off your hike at the trailhead.

If you're camping out and you have to melt snow for cooking, think
about how much water you will need for your dehydrated meals and how
much fuel you'll need to heat the water. Lean toward hot, complex-carb
cooked meals like oatmeal for breakfast and whole-grain pasta or rice
dishes for dinner. Check the directions on your meals and make sure you
have enough fuel and a big-enough pot to prepare them.

Avoid using a water bladder in your pack during cold weather, as the
tubing will inevitably freeze. Instead, carry water and other drinks in an
insulated flask, or in a 2-liter bottle tucked into an insulated bottle parka
attached to your hip belt. In extreme cold, flip the bottle upside-down to
keep the top from freezing over. Keep most of your drinks and food inside
your pack. If you do end up in cold weather with a bladder, try blowing
into the tube periodically—at least every time you take a sip—to prevent it
from freezing up, and tuck the mouthpiece between your skin and clothing to keep it warm.

WINTER TERRAIN AND LAND NAVIGATION

Snow makes its own terrain, which can add a lot of fun and excitement to your trip. It also presents challenges and hidden dangers. Wind and snow can polish windward slopes to a hard, slick crust and form cornices on the leeward sides of ridges. Cornices aren't always obvious, but they extend past stable ground and can collapse if you step on them or fall on top of you as you hike below them. Icy trails can slow you down, especially if you don't have adequate traction for your boots and gear like an ice axe or trekking poles for stability.

Snow and cold can also transform areas that are typically impassable, opening up new routes that don't exist during warmer times of year: a loose, rocky gully becomes a snow-packed couloir to kick-step up, or a lake freezes over, enabling you to cross on snowshoes, spikes, or crampons. Research winter routes to make sure these areas are safe. The time of day you go is also critical. A sturdy snowpack in the morning may be avalanche-prone by midday. Lakes melt out, and marshes that you can float across in snowshoes in the morning can soften into "wallowfests" by afternoon. Likewise, a frozen, rocky slope that's safe for contouring with ice axe and crampons early in the day can become dangerous as the sun warms the rocks. The daily freeze–thaw cycle can cause rocks to pop out beneath your feet and above your head. You might be able to take advantage of the safer snow conditions in the early hours, but plan a different route for the return trip if the terrain is unstable.

Expect to run into a variety of snow conditions, especially at altitude. *Sastrugi* is hard, windswept snow characterized by wave-like ripples. *Snow cups* are areas of bowl-shaped depressions in the snow created during a melt cycle. *Névé* is snow that's partially melted and refrozen into a granular, compacted mass. Different types of snow present unique surfaces to be navigated and an opportunity to test your snow-travel skills. If you are new to backcountry travel on snow, find a mentor to help with your trip planning, route finding, risk assessment, and anchor and belay gear placement, especially on steep terrain and at high altitudes where a mistake can be fatal.

When you're planning a winter outing, take into account the shorter days. With less sunlight you may have to start later and be back to camp earlier to avoid hiking in the dark; with changing terrain, you may have to start very early and so the dark is unavoidable. If you have to be in the dark at some point during your trip, do it in the morning when you're still fresh. If you can, scout out the first part of your hike the day before so you know what it looks like and can follow it more easily in the dark.

Expect winter hikes to take longer, too. Unless you're on skis, it takes more time and effort to trudge through snow in boots and on snowshoes. You can't always take the most direct route, either, and may have to take a longer one to avoid crossing below avalanche terrain.

Snow and wind can create whiteout conditions that make navigation difficult. If you get caught in a snowstorm, don't panic. Rely on your map and compass skills and consider your last known location and your destination to find your way safely. A GPS can be a lifesaver in a snowstorm, especially if you've preloaded waypoints for the route.

WINTER CLOTHING AND GEAR

Dress for the cold and wind and pack extra layers. Start with top and bottom liners and add insulating layers as needed, depending on the temperature. Top with a softshell or hardshell jacket and pants for high winds and precipitation, and always pack a hooded wind- and waterproof jacket that fits over all your upper layers. Bring extra layers for your head, hands, and feet, too.

Wearing a hat, sunglasses, and buff will protect most of your face, but in extreme cold and wind you need to cover every inch of skin. A softshell facemask with holes for your eyes, nostrils, and mouth provides full coverage. Facemasks come in different fabrics, weights, and styles. Before venturing out in freezing temperatures or high winds, test your face-protection system to make sure it's snug, with no open areas where your skin is exposed or gaps where air can sneak in. If your facemask has gaps around the temple area, add a headband or snug cap to seal it off. Add a buff around your neck to pull up over the mouth and nose portions of the facemask.

Some facemasks have very small holes for your nose and mouth; if they restrict your breathing, you may need to widen them by cutting out some of the fabric. For an added layer of protection, smooth a layer of petroleum jelly over your face, neck, and ears before putting on your face protection. The jelly does not have any medicinal qualities that prevent frostbite or sunburn; however, it forms a barrier against moisture that can cool quickly on your skin's surface and lead to windburn and frostbite.

Pack at least one facemask, a winter-weight buff or balaclava, and a snug-fitting cap that covers your ears. For your feet, wear waterproof, mid-rise mountaineering boots and socks or sock layers. If you are particularly susceptible to the cold, you may need insulated boots, and if you'll be wearing crampons, make sure the boots are crampon-compatible. For your hands, a glove combination such as a liner and an insulating glove will keep your fingers from going numb. If you're venturing out into very cold, windy conditions, add a third layer, such as a mitt. Unlike gloves that have separate compartments for individual fingers and thumbs, a mitt has just one or two compartments to decrease the exposed surface area and retain warmth. *Taped mitts* have windproof seams. Wearing mitts limits your dexterity, but on a cold, windy day the extra layer of trapped air and protection from the wind could save your fingers from frostbite. Consider adding chemical warmers for hands and feet to your first-aid kit too.

If you're going to be in snow, add winter gaiters to keep your lower legs dry and keep snow from collecting inside your boots. Depending on the terrain, you may need traction for your feet, too. For icy trails, strap-on spikes work well, and for deep snow, you may need snowshoes

or skis. Before you buy skis or snowshoes for your adventure, do some research to make sure you're getting the right kind for the terrain. For winter mountaineering, avoid snowshoes that are made of fabric, which can tear on rocks. Also avoid complicated buckles; remember, you're going to be putting these on and taking them off in the cold and snow, with gloves on. Look for

Poles and traction keep you upright on slick winter trails.

solid snowshoes with steel traction rows that stand up to rugged terrain. Snowshoes with rails only in the front do not provide enough traction on inclined terrain, especially if you're contouring or "side-hilling" across a slope. Look for dual, parallel rails on each snowshoe and a simple strapping system, and test taking the snowshoes on and off in the store while wearing gloves.

If you usually carry a pen for taking notes on your hike, bring a pencil in case the ink in the pen freezes. Secure everything to yourself or your pack, especially if you're traveling in high winds or on deep snow. A glove that you remove for a moment can be whipped away, and a dropped water bottle, GPS, cell phone, and even a snowshoe can be hard to locate and dig out from under several feet of snow. If these items don't have built-in tethers, make them out of cordelette or use a small carabiner.

HELMETS, CRAMPONS, AND ICE AXES

Helmets aren't necessary on most winter outings, but if you're on a slope where a fall is possible, wear one. The initial fall may not injure you, but sliding downhill at high speed into rocks or a tree could cause a lot of trauma, or kill you.

If you're going to be on hard or steep snow or ice, wear steel or aluminum crampons. They do not provide flotation like snowshoes, but they will give you better traction than snowshoes or strap-on spike traction. Buy crampons that fit the boots you're going to wear with them. Sharpen them with a file as needed, using a light touch on aluminum and a more aggressive one on steel points. To avoid rust, allow crampons to dry completely after every use and oil the metal lightly before putting them away for the season. Metal crampons can transfer cold to your boots, especially boots with a metal shank, and to your feet. You may need to wear warmer socks, sock liners, or even two pairs of socks to combat the cold.

An ice axe is a must for winter mountain travel. The axe's main parts are a long metal shaft with a spike at one end and a curved head with a flattened adze and a pointed pick at the other end. Buy the right-size axe for your body. If you stand straight and hold the axe by the head, the spike should hang down to just above your ankle. The length is important because of how you use the axe for crossing slick or unstable terrain and for self-arrest in case you fall.

Ice axes come in handy for winter hiking, climbing, and mountaineering.

Loop a leash through the carabiner hole at the head of your axe. When the axe is not in use, stow it on the front of your pack or carry it by the shaft with the leash around your wrist. An ice axe can become very cold in your hand; if this is the case, duct-tape a piece of closed-cell foam to the shaft at the point where your hand grips it, for insulation. On sloped terrain, carry your axe at the ready, by the head. In addition to the leash, consider attaching the axe to your pack or to the belay loop of an alpine harness with a bungee, webbing, and carabiner. This way, the bungee keeps the leash short enough so it's out of your way but allows you to extend your arm when you need to. And even if you drop the axe, you won't lose it.

SLEDS

If you have a lot of gear to pack for a winter outing, pulling a sled may make more sense than carrying everything on your back. Strap a duffel to the sled and use webbing to attach the sled to your winter harness. The benefit of pulling a sled is that you can put a lot of weight on it. You can even stick a small portable barbecue grill on one and pull it to your winter campsite, along with frozen meals to cook on it. The con of sled-pulling is that the sled can be cumbersome. If the snow is too soft and deep, the sled may not float on top. If you're pulling a sled across a slope, the sled gives in to gravitational pull, sliding away from you. Attaching a sled to two people—one in front and one in back—can keep it under control. If you want to use a sled, practice with a short outing the first time to get the hang of it, and then decide if it's a piece of gear you'd want to use for longer trips.

AVALANCHE GEAR

If you plan to visit an area where there is any chance at all of avalanches, you will need an avalanche beacon (transceiver), a probe, and a shovel. A beacon sends a signal so that if you're buried, someone else with a transceiver can locate you. It can also receive a signal so if someone else in your party is buried, you can locate them. The probe is used to plunge into the snow to help identify the location of a buried individual, and you will need a shovel to dig them out.

Wear your beacon over your base layer only, under your layers, so that if you're caught in a slide, it isn't ripped from your body. Likewise, store your shovel and probe inside your pack so they're not torn from the outside of your pack. Make sure the batteries in your beacon are fully charged. Though lithium batteries are favored for most outdoor electronics, they do not display a charge the same way alkaline batteries do, so you may think you have fresh batteries even though they could be nearly depleted. Check the manufacturer's site for transceiver battery recommendations. Carry extra batteries for the transceiver and other electronics inside your pack and insulated from the exterior. The cold air will deplete them.

Even if you have all the gear and the training to survive an avalanche, do not underestimate the danger. A transceiver may save you, but more likely, it will only be useful to retrieve your body. A good rule of thumb is to think about the hike before you leave your car and decide whether you'd be comfortable leaving your avalanche gear behind. If the answer is "no," then don't do the hike. Go somewhere else, or go on another day when it's safer.

Get the gear, learn how to use it, and practice with it every season. In the event of a slide, you will not have time to think about what to do. Check for avalanche risk before you head out and be aware of current and changing conditions. The National Operational Hydrologic Remote Sensing Center (NOHRSC) site provides information on precipitation and snow depths, and regional websites like the Colorado Avalanche Information Center (CAIC) site provide detailed information on avalanche conditions.

Even if you're not planning to be in avalanche-prone areas, carry an inclinometer to check the angle of slopes you intend to climb, traverse, or pass below. Slopes between 25 and 50 degrees—with 38 degrees being the sweet spot—are more likely to slide than steeper or less steep slopes. The snowpack also contributes to the likelihood of a slide. If you're approaching a slope within that range and you don't have any information about the avy danger, find another route. Likewise, if you hear the unmistakable, loud cracks of snow collapsing and you're near a slope, get away.

WINTER SKILLS AND TRAINING

A complete discussion of avalanche safety, gear, and training is beyond the scope of this book. If you plan to venture into territory that's susceptible to avalanching, take an avalanche safety course before you go, and refresher courses annually. If you're going to make snow travel part of your regular backcountry lifestyle, consider taking AIARE (American Institute for Avalanche Research and Education) Level 1 and Level 2 classes. Keep in mind that avalanche safety classes are usually taught by and aimed at backcountry skiers, so their advice—especially regarding route planning—may sound odd and

Carrying a shovel, probe, and transceiver is useful for rescuing someone caught in an avalanche, but knowing how to assess and avoid avalanche terrain with proper training is much more critical.

counterintuitive to anyone planning to hike or snowshoe a route. Skiers are looking to ski down open slopes—prime avalanche terrain—while snow hikers can avoid these dangerous inclines and hike through trees and across ridges. Still, much of the advice applies to anyone venturing into snowy territory, and the training is worth the time and cost.

In addition to avalanche training, some basic winter skills and regular practice will make snow travel easier, safer, and more fun. Because these are skills that you won't use during the snow-free season, they're easy to forget. It's a good idea to set a day or a whole weekend aside each year at the start of the season to practice all your snow skills with a group of friends, or you may choose to take a refresher class and field session.

Bootpacking, Kicking Steps, Cutting Steps, Plunge Stepping, and Rest Steps

Knowing how to use your boots and axe on snow creates a secure path for yourself and people behind you. *Bootpacking* is simply packing down the snow with your boots as you walk. You don't have to do anything special—just follow the person in front of you, or the tracks from people who've hiked the path before. When enough people follow the same path, the snow becomes compacted. A bootpacked trail is easier to navigate than one that hasn't been hiked after a big snowfall, so if you don't want to wallow in snow on your winter hikes, look for popular trails that other people have bootpacked for you. Return the favor by improving the path with your own steps.

Kicking steps and *cutting steps* are techniques used on steep slopes. Instead of stepping on the snow, kick your foot into the slope to create a level platform for your foot. You can do this with your boot or cramponed boot. A winter mountaineering boot with a steel shank is best for kicking steps, so the shank—not your toes—takes the brunt of the impact. On very hard snow or ice, you might need an ice axe to cut the steps. If you're following someone else's kicked or cut steps, repeat the kicking motion into the steps to improve them and maintain the same level platform. Do not flatten them parallel to the hillside or you'll create a slippery path for the people behind you on their ascent, and for your own later descent.

Kicking steps in snowshoes is also possible, and you'll appreciate the hinged area of the snowshoe that allows you to do this. After a lot of uphill kick-stepping in snowshoes, your calves may become fatigued from maintaining the flex in your leg to make the kicks. For this reason, some snowshoes have a heel lift—a small bar that sits under your heel, supporting it for such tasks. If you have weak calves or you plan to do a lot of uphill hiking in deep snow, you may want to invest in snowshoes with a heel lift.

Plunge stepping is a technique for walking downhill, accomplished by purposefully plunging your foot, heel first, into the snow to create a solid placement. Finally, practice *rest steps*, where you pause between steps, resting your weight on your feet and allowing your muscles to relax. This gives you small breaks, so you don't wear yourself out.

Ice Axe Use

Ice axes are useful in place of a trekking pole on steep slopes. You can use them in *cane position*—driving the spike end into the snowy hillside as you kick steps up the slope while maintaining three points of contact, with axe in one hand, pole in the other, and your two feet. Axes are also useful as an anchor for belaying other people up a slope. Other types of belay anchors specially made for snow—deadmans and pickets, for example—are available, and you should familiarize yourself with them, but most often you will rely on your axe simply because you are more likely to have one. Setting up and using an axe by itself or backed up with your boot to belay someone downslope from you is a skill that you will want to learn and practice if you plan to do a lot of winter mountaineering. Take a class or engage an experienced mentor to train you, and practice the skill at the start of the snow season.

An ice axe may also be used for *self-belay* and *self-arrest*. If you are crossing particularly icy, snowy, or steep terrain where a slip is likely, keep your axe at the ready so you can engage it immediately to halt your fall. Rather than holding it by the shaft, hold the axe by the head, spike down and adze forward. If you are contouring a slope, use your uphill hand to hold the axe. Using the axe as a cane, drive it firmly into the snow before each step. If you lose your footing, self-arrest by slamming the spike into the ground with your axe hand, grabbing the shaft with the other hand, and quickly sliding that hand all the way to the ground so you have both hands on the axe but don't lever it out of the snow. If your self-belay isn't successful and you go careening down a slope, you'll have to self-arrest by digging the curved, serrated pick end into the snow and putting the weight of your body on it to halt the slide.

The hand position for a self-belay (pick forward) is different than for a self-arrest (adze forward). The thinking behind the self-belay hand position is that resting your palm on the flat adze allows you to drive the spike deeper into the snow. However, if your self-belay fails and you have to self-arrest, it could be more difficult to get your axe into self-arrest position. For this reason, if you're on terrain where a successful self-arrest is crucial for your safety, you may opt to maintain the self-arrest hand position.

Self-belays and self-arrests are skills that require practice on a safe slope with plenty of runout—no rocks, boulders, trees, or cliffs—so you don't crash into boulders or go sliding over the edge. Wear a helmet when you practice and in real-world situations where a slip is possible. Practice self-belays and self-arrests on low-angle slopes. You should be able to self-arrest in four different positions, because when you fall, you have little control over how you will land: feetfirst, facedown; feetfirst, faceup; headfirst, facedown; or headfirst, faceup. The goal is to get yourself in a feetfirst, facedown position by flipping your body over onto your axe and slamming the pick into the ground with your weight over it, which will swing you into a feetfirst position. Find some friends to practice with and take turns. Wear a thick jacket when you practice to avoid skewering yourself with the axe, and practice on easy slopes first to get the hang of the motion before testing your self-arrest skills on steeper slopes. Practice self-belays and self-arrests every year so that if you do fall unexpectedly on a trip, your muscle memory will kick in and you'll be able to stop your slide.

Glissading, or an intentional slide down a hillside, is another good skill to have in snowy seasons. You can glissade in a seated or standing position, though seated is safer and easier. Before you glissade, make sure there is plenty of runout at the bottom of the slope. Anchor yourself into the snow while you get into position and remove your crampons, which can catch in the snow and cause an abrupt stop—maybe even a broken leg. Hold your ice axe with two hands, to your dominant side, spike up and pick down and toward the snow. Your dominant hand should be on the head with your other hand on the shaft. In the seated glissade, be prepared to use the axe as a rudder to steer your slide and as a brake to slow and arrest it—just like a standard self-arrest—and push off, keeping the heels of your feet in the snow to control the speed. If you don't slow or stop before you get to the bottom of the runout, you'll have to flip over and self-arrest. A standing glissade is similar, but instead of sitting, you maintain a standing position.

Glissading can be extremely dangerous because you are basically putting yourself into an uncontrolled slide. However, on low-angle slopes, they provide an alternative to downclimbing, and will get you off a hill fast, which can be useful in the event of a sudden storm or other dangerous situation where you have to make a hasty retreat. If you think you might be doing a seated glissade on a trip, wear water-resistant or waterproof pants, such as insulated mountaineering pants, or pack some rain pants. Practice ahead of time, and never glissade on hard snow or ice, steep slopes, angled slopes that can force you in another direction than the one you are aiming toward, or anywhere that you can't see the bottom of your runout.

WINTER CAMPING AND COOKING

Days are shorter in winter, so you have to either set up camp early or in the dark. Try to plan your trip to get to the campsite at least an hour before nightfall and set up your four-season tent in a safe place. Beware of trees laden with freezing rain that can break overnight. In snow, traditional tent stakes are useless. Instead, use the snow anchors that come with a four-season tent—squares of fabric that look like tiny parachutes. These are also useful when camping on sand, so if you're ever camping in the desert, you'll want to snag these from your four-season tent to use with the three-season one. Dig a hole for each snow anchor, stick them in, and fill with snow to weigh them down. Pack the snow on top of them to make it compact. You can also buy snow stakes that look like small snow pickets—flat, curved stakes with holes in them for more contact with the snow, and more friction. Pound these into the ground at an angle just like a regular stake. In high winds, use the stakes as deadmans, or buried anchors, by digging a small trench for each one and lying it lengthwise (parallel with the ground) in the snow, then burying it. If it's windy or there's precipitation and you need to set up guy lines, but don't have enough snow anchors or stakes, anything stick-like will do: small tree branches, a trekking pole, or an ice axe. Just be sure to dig everything out that you bury when you take down your tent, and don't bury your snow shovel. If you don't have a snow shovel with you, then do not bury your axe. Have something available to dig out the anchors the next day.

Once your tent is set up, establish a bathroom spot away from the tent—preferably a spot that offers some privacy—and another spot in the opposite direction of the tent for shoveling snow to melt for water. Stomp out the trail to the makeshift bathroom so you can find it in the dark. Gather snow in pots, bottles, and bags and set them in the sun to start melting while you finish organizing the inside of the tent and preparing to cook dinner.

As mentioned earlier, melt enough snow for dinner, the next morning's breakfast, and the next day's hike before you turn in for the night. You will not want to do it in the cold of the morning, and waiting until then will delay your start. Cooking in cold temps has its challenges. If you're using a canister stove and your isobutane fuel gets too cold, it won't work. Keep it inside your pack or tent until you need it. A platform for the canister will stabilize it on the uneven snowy surface and keep it off the cold ground, which can help a little. On very cold overnight trips, you may need to invest in a liquid fuel stove. If you have a tent with a vestibule that's ventilated to allow for cooking inside, that's an option, too. Again, never cook in a tent or vestibule that isn't specifically made with proper ventilation for a stove because the fumes could kill you.

Your tent is more likely to get damp inside in the winter. Snow drifts in, or you bring it in on your boots. Try to keep your feet outside the tent while you remove your boots, then bang them together to get the snow off and let them dry in the vestibule. Do not wear your crampons in the tent.

If you do get snow in the tent, brush it out before it melts. If you're car-camping and have a windshield brush handy, that works well. Otherwise, carry a small brush in your pack for this task or just sweep the snow out with your gloved hands. The tent will also get damp inside due to condensation. No matter how cold it is outside, make sure you have some vents open to allow for air circulation. Otherwise, you'll wake up to indoor "snow"—frozen condensation falling inside the tent. Prevent moisture from getting on your sleeping bag or pad, which will make the fabric soggy, cold, and less insulating. A closed-cell foam pad under your inflatable insulated pad provides a waterproof barrier against the bottom of the tent and another layer against the cold ground.

Leave only metal or plastic items outside in the winter, like trekking poles, ice axes, snowshoes, and sleds. Keep everything else in your tent, preferably in your sleeping bag. This includes clothing, electronics, batteries, and fuel. Bring your boots inside the tent before you go to bed to prevent them from freezing overnight. On really cold nights, stick them in a plastic bag (leave the bag open to allow them to dry out) and tuck them into the bottom of your sleeping bag. Squeezing your feet into frozen boots in the morning is nearly impossible and will delay your start while you thaw them out. If your clothes are damp, take them off and sleep with them inside your sleeping bag. The warmth of your skin combined with the absorbing qualities of the bag will dry them overnight. If you have a mesh pocket inside your bag, stash your phone and headlamp there so you can find them in the dark. Outside your bag, keep your FUD, pee bottle, and puffy booties handy, along with a liter of water in an insulated flask or parka for nighttime sips.

The nights are longer in winter and sitting outside in the dark isn't pleasant, so you'll probably be turning in earlier than usual. Use this time to review the next day's route. You can also bring along something to keep you occupied in the tent, like a deck of cards or a book. To save headlamp batteries, consider hanging a small tent candle inside the tent. The soft glow can be comforting, and the flame may raise the temperature a few degrees.

TAKE STEPS

1. Winter hiking and camping isn't for everyone, but don't knock it till you've tried it. Rent a pair of snowshoes from your local retailer, strap them on over some waterproof hiking boots, and take them out for a spin on a local trail.

2. Plan a winter camping trip or one in winter-like conditions where there is snow on the ground. Borrow or rent a four-season tent and get a friend to join you. Make it local so that if you hate it, you can bail.

3. As you get more experience, consider combining your high-altitude and winter skills to plan a high-altitude winter hike or camping trip. Before you go, take a course in avalanche safety and practice your snow travel skills.

Harness, helmet, and steel crampons are standard gear for glacier travel. Geimi Chism's team is geared up to rope up on Mount Olympus, Olympic National Park, Washington.

PHOTO BY NICOLE ALLEN

CHAPTER 23

GLACIER TRAVEL

GLACIER TRAVEL IS a major, yet natural step up from winter hiking and high-altitude mountaineering. Glaciers form when snow lingers on the ground long enough to compress into an ice mass. Unlike temporary snow that melts away with the seasons, glacier snow lasts, growing thicker and heavier until it begins to slowly flow under its own weight. Glaciers aren't permanent, though, and around the world, they have been shrinking in recent decades due to global warming and climate change. Glaciers' movement differentiates them—and more importantly, how you approach them—from traditional snowy terrain. As they compress, buckle, crack, and flow, glaciers form bergschrunds, crevasses, seracs, icefalls, moats, and moraines that require a new skill set.

Glaciers can be found on every continent. Most US glaciers are located in Alaska. If your trips are confined to the contiguous United States, you'll find snowy glaciers in just a few states along the northern Pacific Coast and the Rocky Mountains. Some glaciers, such as Nevada's Wheeler Peak Glacier, are covered in rocks. Rock glaciers may still have ice fields within them and can be very unstable. If you're planning a trip to higher altitudes outside the United States—Canada, the Mexican volcanoes, or Ecuadoran volcanoes, for example—you'll want to do some research to find out if glacier travel is involved.

This chapter is about snowy glaciers. If you want to climb Washington's Mount Rainier, Oregon's Mount Hood, California's Mount Shasta, or Wyoming's Gannett Peak, you will need to understand glacier travel. Much of what you've read to this point, especially in chapters 21 and 22 ("High-Altitude Mountaineering" and "Winter in the Wilderness"), applies to glacier travel. You will be at a high elevation, and even if your trip is in the middle of summer, you will be dealing with the same challenges of winter hiking.

The recommendations in those chapters around weather, health, nutrition, hydration, clothing, sleeping, camping, and cooking hold true for glacier travel. This chapter focuses on terrain, land navigation, gear, skills, training, and accidents. It is a summary of what you need to know, and you should research the subject in more depth and invest in training and practice before going on a trip that requires glacier travel.

GLACIER TERRAIN AND LAND NAVIGATION

A glacier's slow movement creates surface cracks that can stretch apart to form massive openings wide enough to swallow a person or a whole team. Similarly, *bergschrunds* are large cracks at the head of a glacier where it breaks from either adjacent snow that has not compacted into glacier ice or from granular firn that hasn't completely compacted.

On popular routes, crevasses may be marked with *wands*, which are bamboo poles tipped with brightly colored flags. Don't expect these flags to always be in place, though. Expect unmarked crevasses and bergschrunds and be prepared to navigate them.

When crossing terrain that you know to be crevassed, it's important to stay roped to at least one other person and to put some distance between yourself and others on the rope. If you are too close, you could both fall into the same crevasse and there would be no one to get you out. If you allow too much distance or slack in the rope and one person falls in, they could fall a longer distance than is necessary and get seriously injured, or yank other people on the rope team off their feet.

If you come to an exposed crevasse, it's up to you to notify other people on your rope team. Then you have to figure out how to navigate over or around it. You can hike around it, or, if it's narrow enough, you might be able to jump over it. Often, crevasses are hidden under a layer of snow. If the snow's thick and dense enough to support your weight, forming a snow bridge, you may walk over the crevasse without even knowing it's under your feet. Since temperatures drop overnight, snow bridges are firmer in the very early hours. A glacier that appears crevasse-free on an ascent may become much more dangerous later in the day as snow bridges soften and melt out. For this reason, summit attempts that cross glaciers usually start very late at night or early in the morning.

Though crevasses are the most common challenge on glaciers, large blocks of ice known as *seracs* also pose a threat, especially if they come

Geimi Chism and her team hike below a gaping bergschrund at the top of Gooseneck Glacier on Wyoming's Gannett Peak. PHOTO COURTESY OF GEIMI CHISM

GEIMI CHISM is an aerospace engineer who fell in love with mountaineering after watching a documentary on K2. Although she hasn't summited that peak, she spends her spare time climbing in the Rocky Mountain backcountry. She's taught various mountaineering courses, exposing up-and-coming mountaineers to rock, snow, and ice. Geimi's favorite recent climb was to the summit of Wyoming highpoint Gannett Peak. When she's not climbing with friends, Geimi teaches rock climbing to middle-school girls in an afterschool program.

loose and tumble down the mountainside. A serac could crush you or start an avalanche that buries your camp. In areas where glacier ice flows more swiftly than the surrounding ice, such as a steep or narrow section, an icefall may form. *Icefalls* are like frozen waterfalls on a glacier—steep, slick, and often heavily crevassed. Because of the unusual activity of ice and snow, seracs and icefalls are commonly found together.

Moats pose another potential hazard on glaciers. These are large gaps that form in the snow around sun-warmed boulders and along rock walls. Moats can grow wide and deep. Avoid sliding into them and try to find a safe way around them. Established routes may have aluminum ladders set across gaping bergschrunds, crevasses, and moats, but don't count on it. If you have to cross a moat, you may be able to climb down and then out of it. Your team may have to belay each other across.

Finally, *moraines* consist of sediment deposited by glaciers. This can be a combination of mixed-size rocks and gravel lodged in ice and snow. Moraines may be consolidated, but don't trust them. Loose chunks of rock and ice can dislodge, making for uncertain, unstable footing. Proceed over or around them with caution.

GLACIER GEAR

Plan to wear a helmet and crampons on glaciers. You'll also need an ice axe, rope, an alpine harness, webbing, and carabiners to keep you attached to others on your team in case you fall. Add prusiks, which are lengths of cord looped and tied with a double fisherman's knot, or ascenders to get yourself out of a crevasse, and a pulley to set up a C-pulley or Z-pulley system to extract another person from a crevasse. Pulley system setup is beyond the scope of this book but is a skill you should learn and practice before venturing onto a glacier. If you plan to mark the crevasses, you should also bring wands. If you will be ascending especially steep or icy sections, you may need snow anchors such as pickets, and ice anchors such as screws. You may also need to carry avalanche gear.

A short explanation of each piece of gear follows. Before you go on a trip that involves glacier crossings, research the area and try to get a gear list specific to the route. You may not require all this gear, or you might need additional gear not listed. Glacier travel can be remote and require lengthy travel and more gear, so expect to carry more weight.

Helmet: If you own a helmet for rock climbing or ice climbing, use it. You don't need a special helmet for glacier travel. The helmet protects your skull in case you fall on a slope or into a crevasse and from ice- and rockfall. Most helmets have clips for attaching a headlamp. Get the right size for your head and adjust the straps properly so it rests on your head, protects your forehead, and is snug but not binding. In cold temperatures, a fleece cap under your helmet adds a layer of insulation to keep your noggin warm.

Boots: Waterproof mountaineering boots with crampon compatibility are required, with a heel and toe welt for the crampon, plus a steel shank for rigidity when kicking steps. Your boots must be able to hold your crampons, so try them on together before you buy. Stiff boots may seem uncomfortable, but they'll keep your feet from wearing out. Keep in mind that crampons transfer cold from the snow to your foot, so you'll need the right sock or sock system to keep your feet warm. If you are prone to cold feet or are going to an area where you'll be in extreme temperatures for a long time, you may need insulated boots. In the Lower 48, insulated boots are usually not required, but if you travel to Alaska or certain areas overseas, you might need them. Research the route, look for a recommended gear list, and talk to others who have done the trip. Then make the best decision for yourself.

Crampons: Steel crampons are heavier and more durable than aluminum ones. If you're leaning toward aluminum to save weight, just be sure to consider the terrain. Aluminum may not be a good choice for waterfall ice, rocky moraines, or for kick-stepping and front-pointing on steep slopes. Make sure the crampons have anti-balling plates to keep snow from collecting on the bottoms. Choose crampons with a binding system that fits your boots; you don't want them slipping off. To avoid accidents, put your crampons on before you step onto the glacier. Sharpen the points every season and before a big trip.

Skis or snowshoes: Skis and snowshoes are an alternative to crampons that provide float on soft snow and can be safer for crossing snow bridges, but they are also very heavy. The decision to ski or snowshoe should be agreed upon by the team. You need to be moving together on the rope at the same pace.

Ice axe: Like crampons, axes come in both steel and aluminum. Consider the weight and durability and get the right size for your height and arm length. Standing and holding the axe by the head, the spike end should hit near your ankle. Axes are used for cutting steps on hard snow and ice; in place of a trekking pole on steep terrain; in place of an ice tool for climbing steep, hard snow and ice; for self-arresting to save yourself or someone else in the event of a fall; and for a handy boot axe belay. Ice axes are also helpful for probing around crevasses and along corniced ridges to distinguish soft spots from firm terrain.

Avalanche gear: A transceiver or beacon, probe, and shovel, discussed in the last chapter, may be required, depending on the avalanche danger in the area. This can change from day to day and season to season, and should be researched and discussed with your team. If there is no risk, at least carry a shovel for gathering snow to melt at camp, flattening tent pads, and building walls to guard your tent from high winds.

Rope: A dry rope, treated to prevent water absorption, is preferred on glaciers. The treatment keeps the rope from getting soggy, slick, heavy, frozen, and difficult to manage. The rope length depends on how many people are on your rope team. Just two people may only need 30 feet of rope, but a three- or four-person team may need more. You need enough rope to keep the party together while maintaining enough distance so if one person falls, they don't pull everyone down with them. Avoid stepping on the rope, especially while wearing crampons. Allow it to dry completely after a trip and store it away from sunlight.

Alpine harness (bod): Unlike rock-climbing harnesses, alpine harnesses are unpadded, compact, and lightweight. They are designed to keep you attached to the rope and support your weight if you fall. Make sure the harness fits over all your glacier clothing. The leg loops should be easy to unbuckle so you can unlock one and use your FUD to pee without getting out of the harness. Attach other gear such as prusiks, carabiners, and a pulley to the gear loops so you can get to them quickly and easily.

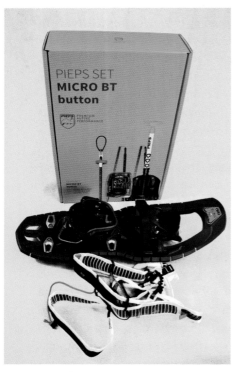

Avalanche safety gear, snowshoes, and a harness may all be required on glaciers.

Chest harness: You can buy a chest harness or just make one from tubular webbing and a carabiner. The chest harness is typically not engaged with the rope unless you're crossing crevassed terrain. If you are, feed the rope from your alpine harness through the carabiner in the chest harness so that if you fall into a crevasse, it will hold you upright. Otherwise, leave the rope out of the chest harness; if you fall on a slope, it can force you into a position that makes it difficult to self-arrest. If you fall into a crevasse without your chest harness engaged, you will at least have it on, and if you can right yourself, you can clip the carabiner onto the rope to hold yourself upright.

Carabiners: Carabiners are used for your chest harness, clipping into the rope, and in crevasse rescue. Figure out what gear you'll need for your trip and then decide how many carabiners you need, and which types—locking or non-locking.

Prusiks or ascenders: Ascenders are mechanical devices for extricating yourself from a crevasse or jugging up a rope (see chapter 24) on a steep section of snow or ice. You can also use two prusik loops—cord tied in a loop with a double fisherman's knot.

Pulley system: The pulley system includes a small pulley, slings, carabiners, and an anchor. The exact number and specifications of each depend on whether you are building a C-pulley or Z-pulley system. This is a complex process that requires research and training beyond this book.

Wands: Bamboo wands can be used to mark crevasses. They're also helpful for retracing a route, especially in whiteout conditions.

Snow anchors: Snow pickets, deadmans, and snow bollards—mounds of snow with webbing strapped around them—are types of anchors commonly used on snow. You can also do a simple body (or hip) belay or boot axe belay. Which type you choose depends on the situation, landscape, and the position of the climbers.

Ice anchors: On hard ice, ice screws and V-threads—where you create a hole in solid ice and thread a runner through and attach a carabiner for an anchor—are options. Anchor-building requires training beyond this book. Learn from a pro, and don't trust a person's life to an anchor unless you absolutely know what you're doing.

SKILLS AND TRAINING

The skills required for safe glacier travel are well beyond the scope of this book. If you're planning to do a well-known peak or route that involves glaciers, consider hiring an alpine guide service that specializes in the route and see if they include a few days of training before the trip. If you want to do the trip unguided, take a formal course on glacier travel and practice your skills. Make sure your team members are also trained, and practice together. This is especially important for developing good communication as a rope team, and for handling emergency situations such as a fall on the glacier or into a crevasse, where teamwork is essential.

The skills you'll need include roping up; identifying and traversing crevasses; communication on the glacier; and navigating around bergschrunds, icefalls, seracs, and moraines. You should know how to use ascenders or prusiks to extricate yourself from a crevasse and how to set up a C-pulley and a Z-pulley to help someone out of a crevasse. Practice these skills with a partner and time yourself. Find a snow berm to hike over and simulate a crevasse rescue. Try to extricate the "fallen party" in under fifteen minutes. Practice falls on steep slopes and self-arresting yourself and others on the rope. Also take time to learn how to set up and use

Geimi Chism pauses on the glacier to admire the sparkling lake below.
PHOTO COURTESY OF GEIMI CHISM

snow anchors, running belays that allow a small team to safely travel from one piece of protection to the next, and boot axe belays. Some of these skills require knowing how to tie certain types of knots. During your formal training, note the types of knots you will need and practice them before your trip. Make sure you can tie them with your gloves on and in the dark.

Practice all of your glacier skills in the weeks leading up to a trip so they're fresh in your mind and muscle memory. And don't neglect physical training just as you would for a peak, including cardio and strength training. If you have a particular climb in mind, research recommended training plans specific to the route. If you are using an alpine guide, they may be able to suggest something for you, or you can find training programs in books and on websites devoted to glacier climbs. Start training early. Give yourself at least three months to get in shape and learn all the glacier travel skills to be safe and successful.

Unlike typical snowfields, glaciers last year-round. Here, the author rests on Gooseneck Glacier during a July climb of Wyoming's Gannett Peak. Though the team carried in glacier gear, conditions that summer—no crevasses or bergschrunds, and snow that allowed for solid kick-steps—precluded the need to rope up. PHOTO BY DOUG HATFIELD

ACCIDENTS ON GLACIERS

If you get into trouble on a glacier on a popular route in the United States during the busy season, you may be able to get help in a reasonable amount of time. However, due to potentially extreme weather conditions and uncertain terrain, you could be waiting a long time for rescue. Before you go, find out the search-and-rescue situation. This can vary widely between areas and seasons, from easy access to a ranger with medical training at base camp to virtually no services at all, especially when visiting certain foreign countries. Whether you are climbing guided or unguided, in the United States or overseas, research the rescue services and plan for the unexpected.

TAKE STEPS

1. If you have tried high-altitude mountaineering, winter camping, and winter hiking and you enjoyed them all, start researching places to put your glacier travel skills to work. Poll your friends to see who else is interested in joining you.
2. Decide whether to go guided or unguided, and hire someone or join a group to get fully trained before your trip. Practice these skills often.
3. Start getting all the gear together that you will need for the trip.

Bethany Burnett leads "Rewritten," a rock climbing route in Eldorado Canyon, Colorado.
PHOTO BY OTINA FOX

CHAPTER 24

ROCK AND ICE CLIMBING

SOME BACKCOUNTRY DESTINATIONS require climbing up and over very steep or vertical terrain with your hands and feet. Learning the basics of rock climbing and ice climbing will help you get past spots that would otherwise limit your opportunities to reach new places. Like the other chapters in this *Next Steps* section, this is not an all-inclusive guide to the subject. It's a brief introduction to climbing so you know what you're getting into and the kinds of gear and skills you'll need. Once you get some practice on vertical terrain, you may discover places that you couldn't reach before. You might even enjoy it enough to pursue rock climbing and ice climbing as stand-alone activities outside of your other backcountry travels.

TYPES OF CLIMBING

The two main types of rock and ice climbing are top-rope climbing (top-roping) and lead climbing. With *top-roping*, the rope is secured to an anchor at the top of the cliff face or ice wall. With *lead climbing*, a climber progresses up a face or wall, setting protection in the form of nuts, camming devices (cams), and slings on rock or ice screws on ice and feeding the rope through the protection.

On a *sport* route, *fixed protection* (or *fixed pro*)—like permanent bolts at the top of a climb and on a wall—give you something to build an anchor on and clip into with a personal anchor system (PAS) or quickdraws (or extenders, which are basically two carabiners sewn into a sling) while you climb. On a *traditional* (or *trad*) route, the climber places active and passive protection in natural features in the rock. Active protection like camming devices are spring-loaded to expand in rock cracks, while passive protection such as chocks, hexentrics (hexes), and nuts are slipped into narrowing or parallel cracks and rely mainly on friction to hold the rope in place. Natural anchors such as trees that are alive, healthy, and firmly anchored in the ground and boulders that are bigger than a refrigerator and not on a slanted surface and can support your weight—*and* the added impact of a fall—may also be used. Do not assume you know what makes good protection or a safe anchor. This is a learned skill and best left to the pros.

CLIMBING GEAR

The essential gear required for climbing is a helmet, harness, climbing rope, belay device, and protection. On rock, you might also want a chalk bag and chalk to keep your hands dry. On ice, you'll need crampons and ice tools. The helmet protects your head from rock- and icefall and lessens the impact in the event of a fall to the ground. The harness holds you in place so you don't fall to the ground. One end of the rope is tied to the harness, the rope is fed through protection or an anchor on the rock face or ice wall, and the other end of the rope goes to a belayer—your climbing partner—who uses a belay device as a braking system to prevent the rope from slipping free and allowing you to fall to the ground.

The helmet, harness, and rope are identical—or similar—for rock and ice (you can use a dry rope for ice climbing if you like). These are not

A climbing rope, helmet, harness, climbing shoes, and quickdraws are basic gear for rock climbing.

Steel-alloy ice tools and crampons facilitate climbing on hard ice.

simply items you can pick up at the hardware store; they're specially made for climbing and tested to withstand the rigors of the sport. Your safety and life depend on them, so they're designed to certain specifications with that in mind.

For both types of climbing, you will need a PAS so you can attach yourself to an anchor at the top of a climb or to protection mid-route, in case you need to pause for a rest or when the climb is threatened, such as by rockfall or an avalanche.

Rock-climbing shoes are flexible so you can flex your feet in different positions to match the terrain, with soles made of material that provides maximum grip on rock. Climbing shoes for advanced climbers may be shaped for specific rock features, such as cracks and narrow ledges. Beginning climbers should get a relaxed sole for basic smearing and edging, climbing techniques that are explained later in this chapter. Tight, binding soles that curl your feet into uncomfortable (even painful) contortions aren't necessary for most climbers, especially those just starting out. On ice, you need boots and crampons for your feet and ice tools for your hands. On mountaineering routes, an ice axe can stand in for one tool. Along with this basic gear, you may also need a variety of slings, webbing, carabiners, and protection, especially if you're a lead climber or the person responsible for setting up anchors.

GO WITH A PRO

Rock and ice climbing are not activities that you can just go out and try on your own, or with inexperienced people who want to "learn as they go." The consequences of a fall are serious. Seek out an expert while you get to know the ropes. Hire a professional guide and tell them your level of experience and your goals for climbing. You may also find an expert among your backcountry buddies, or you can join a climbing group with experienced climbers who are willing to mentor you. Like any backcountry activity, plan to keep yourself safe and don't trust that responsibility to anyone else. Until you know exactly what you're doing, let the person teaching you know just how much you do not know. Otherwise, they may think you know how to put on your harness or tie into a rope when it could be your very first time—and if you get it wrong, you could die.

Your guide or mentor should explain every step in the process, show you how to do it, allow you to do it, and check everything you do along the way, including putting on your harness, tying into the rope, and using your PAS to stay safe. They should communicate with you throughout the climb. The experienced guide should take care of setting up anchors and protection, explain the basic moves to make vertical progress on rock or ice, and make your safety their number-one priority. Even when you become skilled enough to become part of a climbing partnership or team, take it upon yourself to make your—and your partners'—safety your primary concern. You should always check each other's gear, anchors, protection, and anything else that your life depends on during a climb. Do not rush these steps. If you feel like other people are rushing you, tell them that you need to slow down and double-check everything. The consequences of getting it wrong could be fatal.

CLIMBING SKILLS

Starting out, you don't need a lot of skills to climb. Put on your harness, helmet, and climbing shoes (or boots and crampons, for ice). Tighten the harness waist belt and leg loops so they're snug but not binding. Some harnesses require double-backing the strap in the buckle. Make sure it's on correctly so the belt does not slip out of the buckle. Ask an experienced climber to check it for you. After you tie into the rope, ask the person to check your tie-in and the knot. Once you start climbing on your own, maintain this habit of checking your climbing partners' gear and having them check yours on every climb.

Tying into the rope requires a figure-eight knot, which is easy to learn. Measure off a length of rope from your waist to the ground. Tie the figure-eight, then thread the rope through your harness's waist belt and through the loop at your crotch that connects the leg loops. Pull the rope to bring the figure-eight knot close to your waist, then re-thread the knot with the rope end, starting closest to your body and working the rope through the knot and away from you. Make it neat (referred to as "dressing the knot"), with no gaps or twists. You should have some extra rope so the end doesn't slip out of the knot when you weight it. If you have too much extra rope, you can add a fisherman's knot to the end to get the excess out of the way.

Your lead climber or guide will set up the rope and put you on belay. If you fall, the friction of the rope in the belay device—with the belayer's brake hand providing the tension—prevents you from falling more than a foot or so.

CLASSES AND GRADES

No, we're not going back to school. Classes and grades are how the widely accepted Yosemite Decimal System (YDS) categorizes hiking, mountaineering, and climbing difficulty and the potential consequences of a fall. Classes range from Class 1 to Class 5, and within Class 5, grades range from 5.0 to 5.15.

Class 1 is walking on a trail, and Class 2 is walking off-trail and includes using your hands for balance only. Class 3, also known as scrambling, requires using your hands for balance *and* climbing. Class 3 rock does not require edging or smearing. There are good handholds and footholds, and it's often climbed without a rope or helmet, though both are recommended. This is especially true if the climber is inexperienced, if the consequences of a fall are serious, or if there's a possibility of rockfall from above that could knock the climber off the rock.

Class 4 is a step higher than Class 3, and the easiest way to tell the two apart is that you may be able to climb Class 3 facing out from the rock, but Class 4 requires you to face into the rock. Class 4 may also have the potential for serious injury or fatality if you fall, so again, a helmet and rope are a good idea, especially if the rock is unstable. People often get into trouble on Class 3 and 4 routes that are easy to climb up but difficult to descend. *Never* go up anything that you cannot go down.

Class 5 rock routes don't *necessarily* require a rope, but they demand more climbing skill and the consequences of a fall are high, so few people free-climb them. Class 5 is what people typically think of as true rock climbing. The grades are determined by difficulty of the climb, with 5.0 being the easiest and 5.15 the most difficult. Grade 5.10 and above may also be subdivided. When this is the case, the grade is appended with the letter a, b, c, or d. For example, a 5.10b route is more difficult than a 5.10a; a 5.12d route is more difficult than a 5.12c. In addition to the class and grade, routes may also be classified by how long they take to complete and by the recommended protection to safely climb the route. The Roman numerals I through VII denote the time required, with I indicating a climb of an hour or two and VII indicating a climb that takes a week or longer. These are subjective, and the actual time it takes a person to complete a climb could be shorter or longer. Finally, codes G through X indicate the level of available protection, with G indicating good protection and X warning the climber that there is no protection. X may also mean that there is no way to safely protect the route and a fall would likely be fatal. Many mountaineering routes that require climbing tend to be in the Class 3 to Class 5.9 range.

Ice climbing uses three separate grading systems depending on the ice: WI for waterfall ice, AI for alpine ice, and M for mixed ice and rock. The other part of the grading is determined by the difficulty of the route, which takes into account how vertical the climb is and the technical ability required to complete it. Waterfall and alpine ice grades range from WI1 and AI1 to WI7 and AI7; mixed ice grades range from M1 to M15, with M1 being on par as far as steepness with a 5.5 rock climb.

COMMUNICATION

Learn the basic climbing commands so you and your belayer can communicate without confusion.

On belay! Belayer has the rope in the belay device, they have taken the right amount of slack from the rope, they are holding the rope behind the belay device firmly in their hand, and they are prepared to belay Climber.

Climbing! Climber is ready to climb.

Climb on! Belayer hears Climber is ready and gives them the go-ahead.

Up Rope (or Tight)! Climber needs Belayer to take slack out of the rope.

Slack! Climber needs more slack in the rope.

Ready to lower! Climber is sitting in harness and ready to be lowered down from the climb.

Lowering! Belayer is slowly giving the rope slack and lowering Climber.

On rappel! Climber is off the anchor, braking the rope in their belay device, and ready to rappel down from the climb.

Off belay! Climber is on level ground and prepared to untie from the rope.

Belay off! Belayer no longer has Climber on belay. They are not putting any tension on the rope to protect Climber from a fall.

Falling! Climber is about to fall off the face and Belayer needs to ensure a firm grip on the rope and a secure stance because Climber's weight plus the added weight of the fall is going to impact the rope. Belayer needs to halt Climber's fall.

More climbing commands exist, and they vary by climbing area, region, and country.

CLIMBING OUTSIDE

Unlike climbing in a gym, climbing outside doesn't come with molded plastic holds. Different rock types, angles, cracks, ledges, overhangs, and other variations present unique problems for the climber. Likewise, ice has just as many variations, as well as conditions that change with the air temperature. You might initially learn to climb on low-angle walls with fixed protection, but if you plan to incorporate climbing into your backcountry travels, learn all the various climbing techniques to get through the challenges you'll face outside. Both rock and ice climbing entail moving up vertical walls, yet the techniques are different. Even the posture is different, with rock climbers generally keeping their heels up to maintain balance and friction, and ice climbers keeping them down to prevent their feet from becoming dislodged and popping off the wall. If you enjoy climbing, seek out new areas to climb and practice different techniques. Listed below are some of the rock and ice features you might encounter:

Brittle ice: Ice that breaks off easily into "plates" when you insert your tool into it; climbers also call this *dinner-plating*.

The author squeezes into an off-width crack on "Otto's Route," Independence Monument, Grand Junction, Colorado.

Cliff face or crag: Low-angle to high-angle rock wall. Rocky cliffs and crags are usually climbed by smearing, where you rely on balance and friction to make upward progress with hands and feet.

Crack: A crack in the cliff face. The width of the crack determines which part of your body is used for climbing: finger cracks, off-finger cracks or off-hands, hand cracks, off-width cracks, and chimney cracks are increasingly wider, with finger cracks just wide enough to slip a finger into, and chimneys wide enough to stick your whole body into. Methods like jamming and stacking narrow cracks with hands and feet, and stemming wider cracks with arms and legs, are used to maneuver up cracks. With ice climbing, ice tools and crampons must be engaged to maneuver up and around slick, icy features.

Crimps, pockets, and slopers: Small rock features that you can crimp your hands around, stick your fingers in, or press a flat hand or foot on to assist your climb.

Dihedral: Two faces that come together forming an open book–like feature at angles narrow enough to stem across both faces.

Flake: A large flake of rock that can be climbed via a lie-back motion, by holding onto the flake edge with your hands and shuffling across the rock face.

Ice wall: Cliff face or crag covered in natural or farmed (artificially created) ice. Ice formed from hardened snow is called alpine ice. Formed from frozen water, such as a waterfall, it's called water ice. When a lot of icicles form together, the resulting formation is chandelier ice. Climbers swing or place ice tools on and in the ice and kick-step or front-point with their feet to secure themselves in position and make upward progress on a wall.

Jug: Large feature that's big enough to grab to pull yourself up. *Jugging* also refers to moving up a rope with an ascender.

Ledges: Ledges are horizontal features jutting from a rock wall. They can be just thin enough to get a finger, toe, or ice tool over, or wide enough to walk on. On very narrow ledges or rock crystal, you can stand on the edge of your shoe rather than the sole, a technique known as *edging*. Approaching a wide ledge from below, a rock climber can *mantle* onto a ledge by pressing both palms on top to hold their weight, then swinging or lifting their feet up and onto the horizontal surface.

Mixed climbing: Climbing on a combination of ice and rock.

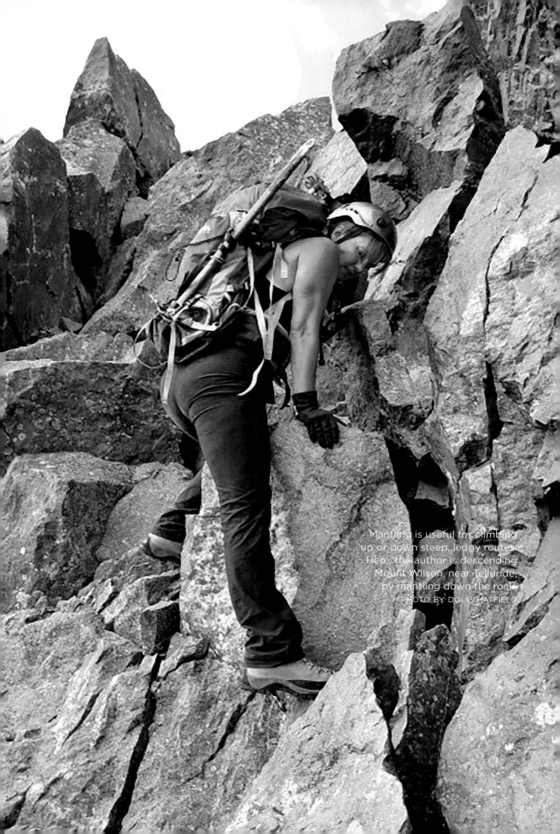

Mantling is useful for climbing up or down steep, ledgy routes. Here, the author is descending Mount Wilson, near Telluride, by mantling down the rock.
PHOTO BY DOUG HATFIELD

GETTING DOWN

Once you've reached the top of a climb, you have two options for getting down: the same way you came up, or by another route. If you're going down the way you came up, you can either downclimb, be lowered, or rappel. *Downclimbing* is the reverse of climbing, and it's more difficult. You can't always see your feet or what's below you, so it's hard to find hand and foot placements. People who go climbing without gear can get into a bad situation by climbing an easy route only to realize they do not have the skills to retreat, and without a rope and protection, there is nothing to catch them if they fall. Downclimbing is a good skill that can come in handy. Practice on a rope with a belayer, and avoid downclimbing technical routes without protection.

More often climbers can just ask their belayer to lower them by using the proper climbing commands. From a seated position in the harness with feet flat on the wall, control the lowering by walking down the wall and giving your belayer instructions to either lower you a little faster or slower. You should maintain control while being lowered and stay tied into the rope until you are on level ground.

Rappelling is another way to get down from a cliff. You essentially belay yourself by braking a single or double rope strand that's anchored safely to fixed protection or a solid, natural anchor and threaded through your belay device. The Hollywood-style rappels you see in the movies are mainly for show. In the real world, you should not put undue stress and strain on a rope by swinging out, or damage delicate rock and ice faces by slamming your feet into them. Rappelling gets you down faster than downclimbing or lowering, but it should still be controlled. Before you rappel, make sure there is a stopper knot at the bottom of the rope so you don't accidentally rappel off the end. Alternatively, you can ask your climbing partner to give you a "fireman's belay," where they hold the end of the rope taut to prevent you from rappelling too quickly, in a freefall.

BELAYING

Typically, there are two active participants in a climb: the climber and the belayer. The climber's job is obvious—they tie into a rope and climb a wall to a point where the rope is anchored. But the rope isn't actually tied to an anchor; it's fed through carabiners that are attached to the anchor, and the other end of the rope is managed by the belayer. With the help of a belay device and using their grip on the rope as a brake, the belayer takes up the

The author prepares to rappel from Independence Monument, Grand Junction, Colorado.

slack in the rope as the climber ascends, pays out more rope as the climber descends, and keeps the rope from slipping through the anchor if the climber falls, controlling the fall and preventing the climber from hitting the ground. Depending on their position and weight compared to the climber, the belayer might anchor themselves to the ground or to the wall so they don't get knocked off their feet or lifted into the air if the climber falls.

Knowing how to safely belay your climbing partner is a critical skill. Have an experienced climber teach you, and practice with them backing you up. You can also learn in a climbing gym; in fact, most gyms require that you get "checked out" on belaying before they allow you to climb. This will teach you the basic skills, but remember: Outdoor belaying comes with even more responsibility. You have to keep an eye on your climber, but you also have to be aware of changing weather, temperatures, and conditions of the rock or ice. A good belayer isn't distracted by other people at the base of the cliff. They maintain clear communication with the climber, and protect the rope, too. In a climbing gym, this is less of an issue; when you're outdoors, you might have to deal with passersby and their kids or dogs. It's important to stay focused and remember that if the climber gets in trouble on a climb, they are counting on their belayer to protect them.

KNOW YOUR KNOTS

Attaching your harness to a climbing rope, connecting ropes together, and tying prusiks, slings, anchors, protection, and other climbing gear requires specific knots. If you use the wrong knot, it may not function the way you need it to; it could even come untied. Learn the basic knots and their uses and practice them, adding more knots to your repertoire as you advance in your climbing skills and responsibilities.

At a minimum, learn to tie a figure-eight knot. You'll need to know this to tie into the rope. Knots to learn include the following:

> **Autoblock:** To back up a rappel in case the device jams and to increase friction and slow your rappel
> **Double-Fisherman's Knot:** For tying ropes together and tying the ends of cordelette together to make a prusik loop
> **Figure-Eight:** For tying into the rope
> **Figure-Eight on a Bight:** For tying into an anchor
> **Klemheist Knot:** For prusiking up a rope
> **Munter Hitch:** May be used in place of a belay device for rappelling and belaying

The author seconds the route on Castle Rock North, removing quickdraws placed by the lead climber and pulling a second rope up for another climber.

- **Prusik Knot:** For prusiking up a rope
- **Square Fisherman's Knot:** For tying two ropes together
- **Stopper Knot:** Tied into the ends of a rappel rope to prevent a person from accidentally rappelling off the end of a rope
- **Water Knot:** For tying webbing, usually into a loop

Many more knots exist, and if you pursue climbing, you will want to learn and practice them.

ADVANCED SKILLS

Again, this chapter is merely an introduction to climbing. If you enjoy it, you'll want to learn how to second a climb, which is following a lead climber and cleaning (removing) the protection set by them; how to set up anchors; how to lead climb; how to create V-threads and place ice screws in ice; and how to place quickdraws in fixed pro on sport routes, and cams, chocks, hexes, and nuts in rock on trad routes.

Climbing can be extremely dangerous, especially if you're careless or don't know what you're doing. Gear failures are rare, and accidents usually occur when a climber simply isn't paying attention or overlooks a basic safety precaution, such as checking their gear to make sure they're properly tied into a rope, checking an anchor to make sure it's secure, or failing to anchor themselves at the top of a cliff face and stepping or slipping off. Natural occurrences such as rockfall and ice collapses can also put a climber in danger. It is not a sport to be taken lightly. Yet, climbing opens a whole new world of outdoor opportunities. Even if you don't plan to pursue it as a stand-alone sport, at least learn enough to get you past the typical vertical obstacles you're bound to encounter as you expand your adventures beyond the beaten path.

TAKE STEPS

1. Before you buy any climbing gear, hire a guide who can loan you all the gear for your first climb so you can decide if it's a skill you want to pursue.
2. If you enjoy it, start buying your own gear and find a climbing group of experienced climbers who are willing to allow you to join them. Be crystal-clear about your lack of experience and ask them to check your gear every time you climb.
3. Find someone qualified to teach you to belay and practice.

Treks, climbs, and alpine adventures outside the United States take more planning and sometimes more training. Here, the author enjoys the Veintimilla Summit of Chimborazo, Ecuador.
PHOTO BY DOUG HATFIELD

CHAPTER 25

INTERNATIONAL TRIP PLANNING

ONCE YOU'VE GOTTEN the hang of planning local trips and the skills to do them, you may want to venture out of state and, eventually, out of the country. You can go higher in Africa, cross a glacier in Mexico, rock climb in Europe, or go ice climbing in South America. You may even want to climb in the Himalayas.

An overseas trip takes more preparation and costs more, too. Give yourself plenty of time to research the area and the route, set your expectations based on what you learn, and expect the unexpected. No matter how much you prepare yourself, new countries, cultures, and people are sure to surprise you. Hiking, camping, climbing, and mountaineering in a foreign land can be a life-changing adventure.

WHERE AND WHEN TO GO

Where you go depends on your goals and preferences. Is there a special place you've read about or seen in photographs and always wanted to visit? Are you working on a goal, like continental or country highpoints? Do you want to up your game by going higher than it's possible to go in the United States? Take all of this into consideration, come up with a few options, and start doing some research.

One important factor is timing. Seasons and weather in other countries don't always line up with what you're used to. For example, in the southern hemisphere, the seasons are flipped. So if you were planning on taking a week off in July to climb the Ecuadoran volcanoes, you may want to rethink your schedule. Another consideration is the different timberlines. If you are traveling to another country with plans to climb and set up camp below tree line, don't assume it's the same elevation as the area where you live. Timberlines vary by thousands of feet in the United States and abroad.

Read guidebooks about specific countries and locations, talk to people who've been there, and go online to discover the best times to visit your potential locations. See if their recommended dates line up with your vacation days. Then start planning.

GUIDED OR UNGUIDED

You can do most trips either guided or unguided. If you decide to go with a guide, the level of services they offer can vary. In general, the more you are willing to pay, the more they do for you. American guiding companies can be very convenient to work with. The communication and payment can be easier, and since they deal primarily with other Americans, they have a good idea of your expectations.

Alternatively, you can hire a guide located in the country you're visiting. Going this route also has its advantages, because you will likely be able to enjoy a more cultural experience. Qualified local guides know the area better than anyone. Also, hiring local means putting money into the country's local economy; depending on where you're going, some cities and countries rely heavily on foreign dollars.

If you do hire someone, find out exactly what you are getting for your money. If you book with a guide—American or foreign—you are usually responsible for your own transportation costs to and from the other country. You may also be responsible for your own transportation in the country you're visiting, as well as costs for food and shelter, such as hotels, motels, and fees (if any) for huts.

However, some guides cover all or most of your costs for a flat fee. This includes transportation from the airport to your hotel, motel, or hut; meals; a guide to get you to the trailhead and back; and a hiking, climbing, or alpine guide for treks, climbs, and mountaineering trips.

Alternatively, you can go unguided and do all the planning and arrangements yourself. This means getting permits; managing transportation; booking hotels, hostels, huts, or campsites; purchasing gear that you didn't bring with you on the plane; and doing your own route finding.

If you aren't comfortable enough in your skills, or you feel like you might need some help getting around and communicating but you don't want to hire a guide, you can go with an unguided group that has an experienced leader. Many hiking groups organize several overseas trips a year. This can also be a very affordable option because you are able to get a group rate on certain services.

Finally, some locations require that you hire a porter or guide. For example, if you want to climb Kilimanjaro, you have to hire a registered, licensed guide. Before you choose one, do your homework. Read the reviews and talk to people who have used their services. Not all guiding companies treat their porters and alpine guides well, so make sure you are going with an ethical company.

COST

The cost of an overseas trip varies wildly, from a few thousand dollars to tens of thousands of dollars. Remember, you're paying for airfare, transportation, accommodations, food, and beverages. There may be climbing fees and access fees, too. If you're going guided, you have to pay for the services of all the people who help to arrange your trip and guide you. You may want to get insurance for your trip, too, such as travel insurance, international health insurance, hazard insurance, and rescue insurance. And don't forget to add tips to your budget. Just like in the United States, in foreign countries the people who provide services—such as food preparation and service, transportation, and trekking, climbing, and alpine guide services—usually get just a fraction of the money you pay the company.

GEAR AND CLOTHING

The gear and clothing you need for a trip depends on the trip, the season, and the weather. If you're going unguided, some thorough research will go a long way toward ensuring a more pleasant trip. If you're using a guide, first, defer to them. Most guiding companies will provide certain gear, such as ropes for climbing and glacier travel, and will give you a list of the gear and clothing you will need to bring yourself. In addition, do your own research. A guide's list is intended for the average traveler. If they recommend a certain type of boot and you know you hike hot or cold and those boots won't work for you, then talk to them about it and see if you should wear different boots.

TRANSPORTATION

Find out what you can and cannot bring on the plane with you. For example, you will not be able to bring fuel for your stove, so if you're carrying a stove in your checked bag, find out if the fuel it takes is available in the country you're visiting. Some other items you may not be able to bring or you will have to package a certain way include batteries, crampons, ice tools, and ice axes. Obviously, you will not be able to take all of your clothing and gear as carry-ons. However, be sure to carry on your boots, a pair of socks, and any other clothing or gear that you will not be able to replace if your baggage is lost en route to your destination. You may be able to buy new boots, but you will not have time to break them in before your big trek or climb. Stick them in your carry-on bag along with your favorite socks, and know that at least your most important item will arrive with you. Line up your in-country transportation ahead of time, if you can. If your guide isn't going to pick you up, research taxi services, buses, and other public transportation.

FOOD AND WATER

A guiding company may provide some—or all—of your meals. If they do, let them know about any food allergies or preferences that you have.

If you're responsible for any of your meals, research markets and restaurants ahead of time, if possible. To be on the safe side, stick to foods you're used to eating before your outing and save the local cuisine for later. The day before a big trip isn't the time to experiment with new foods. Also, find out about the water situation. Not all countries have potable tap water, so you may have to purchase bottled water. If the tap water isn't potable, then don't let any of the water coming out of the sink, showerhead, or bathtub faucet get into your eyes, nose, or mouth either. It could carry harmful bacteria or parasites.

If you're doing a day hike you can carry bottled water, but if you're doing a multiday trip, you may be getting your drinking and cooking water from streams and other sources. Find out the best method for treating the water and come prepared with a filter or chemical treatment, such as iodine or chlorine dioxide tablets. Make sure you have enough for the whole trip.

TRAINING

Training for an overseas trip is no different than training for a local one, unless you're going to higher altitudes than you're used to. Find a training plan specific to the trek or climb and start training early, even months in advance. If it's higher than you're used to, train for altitude. If it's longer or more strenuous, start doing increasingly longer, harder hikes. If technical skills are involved, take a class specific to the skills required and practice regularly in the months leading up to your trip.

LOGISTICS

Make sure your passport is valid, and if it isn't, get a new one. Research the area you're going to well in advance to see if any other paperwork or documentation is required. You may need permits or reservations for some areas. You may need inoculations, too. Other matters to look into include cell phone coverage and money, including cash and credit or debit card use.

Write up a trip plan just as you would do for a local hike. Include your itinerary; contact information; the names, addresses, and phone numbers of places you're staying; and any other trip details. Leave a copy at home with someone you trust and carry the other one with you. This way, if you lose your phone, you will still have access to this important information.

Look for guidebooks, websites, and maps that describe the area and study them ahead of time. Try to find people who have already done the trip; they may have some insight for you about the route, terrain, shelters (like huts) that you may be staying in, and recommended gear and clothing.

SAFETY

Pickpockets and theft can be a problem in some countries. Don't carry a wallet, and if you carry a handbag, don't keep any cash, cards, tickets, or your passport in it. Instead, keep all your valuables in a pouch inside your clothing. Make two copies of your passport and leave one at home with someone you trust so that if you lose yours or it's stolen, you can call them and get them to scan it and send it to you. Take the other copy with you and carry it in your pouch at all times. In some countries, you could be stopped by authorities and asked to produce it. When using public transportation or hanging out anywhere there's a crowd, hang onto your handbag, jacket, and anything else that contains anything you can't afford to lose. If your hotel has a safe, ask them to hold your passport for you there. If you're going to be using a debit or credit card overseas, let your bank know so that they will approve your purchases. Otherwise, when you try to pay for something, your bank may reject the purchase.

CULTURE

Before you visit a country, study the culture. Try to learn some of the language. Find out what people eat there and how they dress. Learn some of the holidays and the customs. While you're there, try to learn more. International travel for adventure can be expensive, but it can also be unforgettable. It can change how you see the world and how you see your own life, back in the States. If you have the time and money, include international trips in your plans.

Becoming a skilled woman in the wild doesn't limit you to your closest state park or national forest. There are wild places everywhere, waiting for the thoughtful adventurer who treads lightly, shares generously, and welcomes the challenges while respecting the beauty found in every corner of the world.

Index

gas (burps and farts), 89
gastrointestinal illness, 103
gear storage, 39
glacier glasses, 190, 198
glaciers, 213, 214, 215, 216, 217, 218, 219, 221
glacier travel, 30, 79, 212, 213, 214, 216, 219, 220, 221, 241
global positioning system (GPS), 5, 23, 29, 35, 69, 98, 99, 110, 113, 118, 119, 120, 121, 122, 123, 125, 127, 135, 141, 144, 145, 163, 174, 201, 202
glove leashes, 190, 202
gloves and glove liners, 15, 16, 18, 19, 21, 91, 189, 198, 199, 202, 210, 220
goals, 4, 104, 136, 165, 167, 168, 169, 170, 171, 178, 181, 226, 239
goal setting, 167, 168, 169, 170, 180
goggles, 93, 133, 190, 198, 199
Gore-Tex, 12, 13
graupel, 133, 197, 198

H

hardpan, 128
hardshells, 14, 15, 189, 201
harnesses, 36, 79, 190, 204, 216, 218, 224, 226, 227, 229, 233, 235
hats, 16, 17, 19, 21, 22, 33, 35, 91, 92, 93, 101, 201
headaches, 60, 81, 87, 88, 101, 105, 188
headbands, 17, 82, 84, 201
headlamp, 7, 22, 23, 34, 48, 78, 80, 127, 182, 211, 216
heat exhaustion and hyperthermia, 101
helmets, 25, 29, 30, 36, 142, 203, 208, 212, 216, 224, 226, 227
high-altitude cerebral edema (HACE), 188
high-altitude flatus expulsion (HAFE), 89
high-altitude mountaineering, 88, 187, 188, 189, 190, 191, 192, 193, 194, 195, 213, 221

high-altitude pulmonary edema (HAPE), 188
highpointing, 169, 171
hiking boots, 11, 12, 47, 211
hiking shoes, 10, 11, 12, 90
hydration, 22, 28, 33, 35, 56, 59, 62, 64, 83, 90, 189, 199, 214
hygiene, xii, 77, 82
hyperthermia, 92, 101
hyperventilation, 105, 188
hypothermia, 92, 198
hypoxia, 191

I

ice ax-boot belay, 219, 220
ice axes, 25, 29, 37, 78, 137, 190, 194, 200, 203, 206, 207, 208, 209, 210, 216, 217, 219, 220, 225, 242
ice climbing, 30, 36, 216, 223, 224, 225, 226, 228, 229, 231
ice-climbing grading systems, 228
icefalls, 213, 215, 219
ice screws, 216, 219, 223, 237
illnesses, 87, 88, 90, 95, 98, 99, 100, 101, 103, 104, 105, 187, 188, 189
injuries, 87, 88, 90, 91, 95, 98, 99, 100, 102, 103, 105, 159, 195, 198, 227
inserts, sole, 12
insulating layers, 9, 14, 189, 197, 201
international trip planning, guided and unguided, 239, 240, 241, 242, 243, 244

K

kicking steps, 131, 200, 206, 216, 217, 221, 231

L

land navigation, 23, 109, 110, 111, 112, 113, 114, 115, 116, 117, 118, 119, 120, 121, 122, 123, 124, 125, 145, 191, 200, 214
layering, 9, 10, 13, 14, 15, 16, 17, 18, 19, 92
lead climbing, 223

About the Author

Susan Joy Paul has traveled around the United States and beyond to 47 hot springs, more than 150 waterfalls, and to the summits of more than 700 peaks. Her memorable adventures include hikes and climbs on the Mountaineer's Route on Mount Whitney, the East Arête on Mount Russell, Otto's Route on Independence Monument, the Emmons Glacier on Mount Rainier, the Gooseneck Glacier on Gannett Peak, the Jamapa Glacier on Pico de Orizaba, the Ayoloco Glacier on Iztaccihuatl, and the Whymper Route on Chimborazo. When she's not outside, she's at her desk writing guidebooks to Colorado's great outdoors. Susan lives independently in Colorado Springs, Colorado.

The author on Tres Orejas, New Mexico